MARK CANDELARIA

HOMES

Mark B. Candelaria and David M. Brown
Edited by Tiffany Candelaria

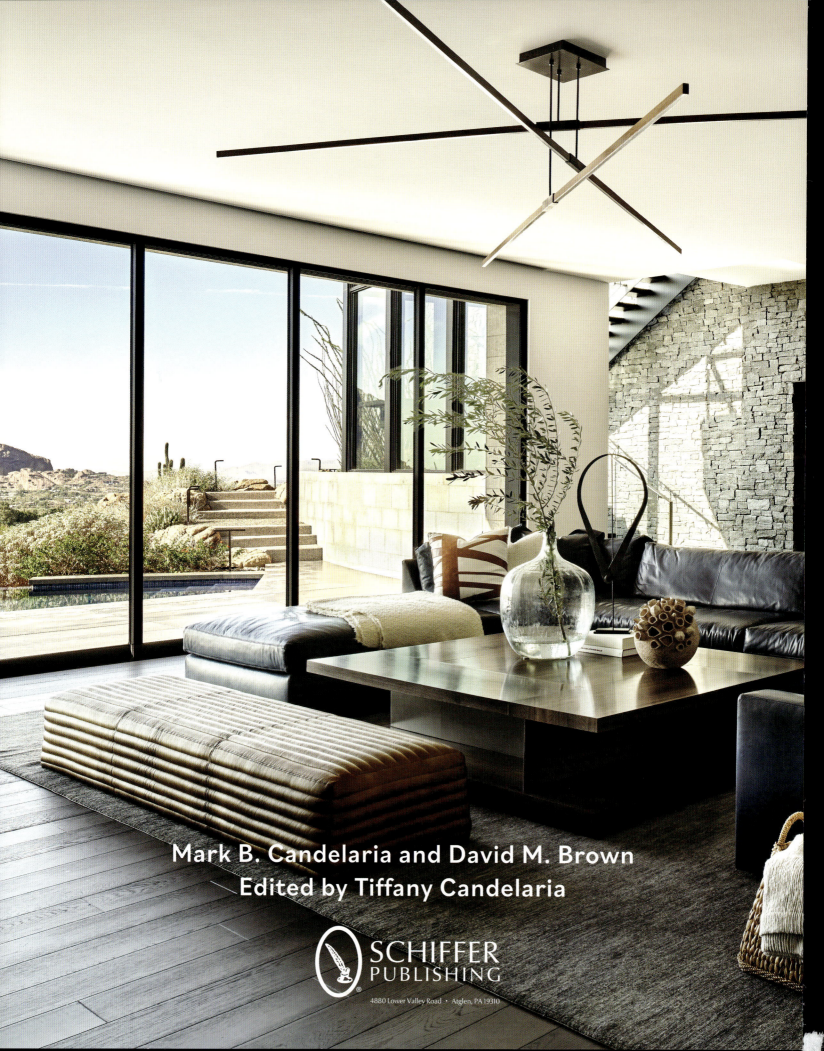

Mark B. Candelaria and David M. Brown
Edited by Tiffany Candelaria

SCHIFFER PUBLISHING
4880 Lower Valley Road • Atglen, PA 19310

MARK CANDELARIA HOMES

Other Schiffer Books on Related Subjects:

Four Seasons of Entertaining, by Shayla Copas,
ISBN 978-0-7643-5731-2

Concrete Houses, by Steven Huyton and Cheryl Weber,
ISBN 978-0-7643-6277-4

Anatomy of a Great Home, by Boyce Thompson,
ISBN 978-0-7643-5465-6

Copyright © 2023 by Mark Candelaria

Library of Congress Control Number: 2022932675

All rights reserved. No part of this work may be reproduced or used in any form or by any means—graphic, electronic, or mechanical, including photocopying or information storage and retrieval systems—without written permission from the publisher.

The scanning, uploading, and distribution of this book or any part thereof via the Internet or any other means without the permission of the publisher is illegal and punishable by law. Please purchase only authorized editions and do not participate in or encourage the electronic piracy of copyrighted materials.

"Schiffer," "Schiffer Publishing, Ltd.," and the pen and inkwell logo are registered trademarks of Schiffer Publishing, Ltd.

Edited by Tiffany Candelaria
Designed by Molly Shields
Front cover photo by Werner Segarra
Back cover photo by Bradley Posey

Type set in Bilo/Cambria

ISBN: 978-0-7643-6521-8
Printed in India

Published by Schiffer Publishing, Ltd.
4880 Lower Valley Road
Atglen, PA 19310
Phone: (610) 593-1777; Fax: (610) 593-2002
Email: Info@schifferbooks.com
Web: www.schifferbooks.com

For our complete selection of fine books on this and related subjects, please visit our website at www.schifferbooks.com. You may also write for a free catalog.

Schiffer Publishing's titles are available at special discounts for bulk purchases for sales promotions or premiums. Special editions, including personalized covers, corporate imprints, and excerpts, can be created in large quantities for special needs. For more information, contact the publisher.

We are always looking for people to write books on new and related subjects. If you have an idea for a book, please contact us at proposals@schifferbooks.com.

This book is dedicated to the twelve clients whose homes are featured, who trusted our team to create their most intimate space, their home. And to cowriter David M. Brown and to my daughter, Tiffany Candelaria, who quarterbacked the production of this book.

CONTENTS

8 *Foreword*
10 *Introduction: A Life from Architecture*

16 CLEMMENSEN / GERDTS AND MCKINNEY RESIDENCE—
Transitional Style
- 34 HALIBUT PUTTANESCA

38 MESSMER RESIDENCE—
Santa Barbara at Mummy Mountain
- 50 GRILLED PEACH, PROSCIUTTO, GOAT CHEESE, AND TRUFFLE HONEY PIZZA

54 SILVERLEAF ESTATE—
Tuscan-Inspired Farmhouse in the Scottsdale Foothills
- 70 HOMEMADE PASTA

75 ITALIAN-MEDITERRANEAN VILLA—
A Repository for Art
- 86 BRAISED SHORT RIBS

90 HISTORIC JOHN M. ROSS TUDOR HOME—
Escape to the English Countryside
- 102 SOUTHWEST-STYLE BEEF WELLINGTON

106 WYSEL RESIDENCES—
Rural Mediterranean in Coastal California
- 118 PORCHETTA WITH SALSA VERDE

122 GAGE RESIDENCE—
Spanish Colonial at Silverleaf
- 130 TIRAMISU

134 LANGE RESIDENCE—
Compass Point to Camelback
- 144 FETTUCINE VONGOLE WITH CHORIZO

148 SCHULTZ RESIDENCES—
Two of a Kind in Paradise Valley
- 164 HERB-CRUSTED SMOKED PRIME RIB AND STEAMED LOBSTERS

168 JOHNSON RESIDENCE—
Hillside Contemporary
- 184 MARK'S SPANISH PAELLA

190 LERNER RESIDENCE—
European Villa at Desert Mountain
- 202 BEEF TENDERLOIN WITH HONEY-GLAZED CARROTS

206 LARRY FITZGERALD RESIDENCE—
French Manor Estate
- 224 BEEF POT ROAST WITH MUSHROOM RISOTTO

FOREWORD

Larry Fitzgerald. *Photo courtesy of Blair Bunting*

Candelaria Design staff at the Fitzgerald Residence. *Photo courtesy of Duane Darling*

Mark takes an artist's approach to his profession. He is a sculptor who converts visions and ideas onto a set of drawings that evolve into a three-dimensional structure—a home. He performs his craft with intuition and precision, while emphasizing the principles of classical form and functionality.

When I first met with him to plan the design of my own house, he explained his design process in a way that resonated with me: "Actually," he said, "you will be the architect, and I will be the instrument through which you will bring your vision to reality." I thought his approach would fit well with the way I think about what I wanted in my home.

Mark noticed the little things in our discussions, taking notes so that he could recall what was required to deliver my desired result. He inquired about my interests, including travel, food, and music, to create a home that would reflect my needs, while incorporating aesthetics, architecture, and design in the process.

From the outset, I knew that I wanted my home to be a respite from the complexities of life, a place of quiet tranquility. I soon realized that I also wanted a home with timeless architecture, much like the centuries-old houses in Europe, which are rich and elegant, yet current. While I had a clear idea of the things that were important to me in a home, I did not know exactly how my objectives would be translated into physical form. Mark and his team, primarily partner Meredith Thomson, understood what I wanted and delivered it.

They relied on the natural environment to help achieve the sanctuary I desired. Their design incorporated my interest in beautiful gardens and captured my property's scenic vistas. The home was designed for people to move easily from space to space, while remaining functional and practical. Mark and Meredith had many creative solutions to address my wishes and concerns. They invested the time to ask and learn how I live and how I would like to live in my new home.

As I spent more time with Mark and we discussed the details of my home, I would often recall our initial conversation and the description of his role as an instrument. This characterized my experience with Mark. All too often the day-to-day issues relating to building a home can become tiresome and even tedious. Mark helped make it fun, and I will always be grateful for the opportunity to work with him and look forward to our next project together.

—Larry Fitzgerald, future Hall of Fame NFL wide receiver

INTRODUCTION
A Life from Architecture

I knew I wanted to be an architect when I was four years old. I had never met an architect, and I didn't have any idea what an architect truly did; I just knew I liked to draw floor plans and then build these creations with the Legos my parents gave me for Christmas. I grew up in Denver, Colorado, in the early 1960s, when a lot of new construction was underway right around the corner from our home. We had a large field behind our home that became my canvas for building forts from the scrap lumber I gathered from nearby jobsites, and for building imaginary subdivisions of my Lego-inspired homes.

I took drafting classes in high school and pre-architecture classes at the University of Colorado, and later took some architecture classes at Arizona State University. Although I was accepted into the School of Architecture at ASU in 1981, I never formally enrolled and instead became the draftsman for one of my professors, the late George W. Christensen, FAIA. Thus, I learned my craft in the old apprenticeship manner, eventually passing the registration exams to become a licensed architect in 1992.

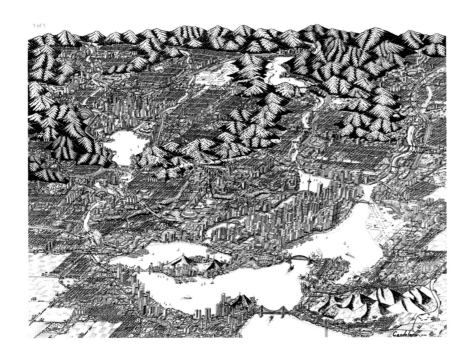

Mark Candelaria in his office. *Photo courtesy of Diana Elizabeth*

Mark's imaginary city, drawn in 1980

After an eighteen-year career with my former professor and mentor, I opened Candelaria Design Associates in 1999 in Arizona. Our firm focuses primarily on high-end residential work, and our repertoire now spans nationwide and includes a diverse gamut of styles.

This book focuses on our work from 2010 through 2020. During that time, three amazing women became my partners: Evelyn Jung; Meredith Thomson, AIA; and Vivian Ayala, who resigned in 2021. Her spot has been filled by our associate of sixteen years, Tim Mathewson. Our principals and our entire team have all contributed in their unique way to the success of this firm. We have now designed hundreds of homes and been named #1 Residential Architecture Firm by Ranking Arizona for eleven years in a row. This book features twelve of my favorites from the past decade, paired with one of my recipes that resonates with each home. We selected these twelve homes because either the home, the client, or both significantly influenced our firm and its direction. At the same time, we recognize that every project we have had the honor to work on has had an impact on the direction of our ship.

Mark and his mentor, George Christiansen (*left*) at their Enchantment Resort project, 1987

Firm principals (*left to right*): Meredith Thomson, Tim Mathewson, Evelyn Jung, Mark Candelaria. *Photo courtesy of Carl Schultz*

The creation of these homes has taught and inspired us, and our mission is the same for our clients: to have our designs inspire and enhance their way of living every moment of their lives. The creation of a home is not about drawing a set of plans. Our philosophy is that this journey should be a pleasant experience that gets fused into the bricks and mortar of the home as its spirit. We do this through a collaborative design process with our clients; through our tours to Italy, Spain, and locally; and through cooking and enjoying fabulous dinners with them along the way, and many times long after their project is completed.

Our time, as they say, is short. Now is all that matters. We have only one journey; that journey is now, and this book is my opportunity to share my heart and soul with readers. Thus, I welcome you to a taste of the past ten years with these twelve homes and twelve accompanying recipes. Please join us on our journey of inspiring living—in Candelaria Style.

—Mark Candelaria

Candelaria Tour Italy 2013, at the Villa San Michele in Florence. These architectural, culinary, and scenic experiences are rich sources of design inspiration.

Client project dinner at the Candelaria Design Studio

Candelaria Tour Spain 2018, enjoying Basque cheesecake in San Sebastian

Mark in the Clemmensen / Gerdts and McKinney billiards room. *Photo courtesy of BradleyWheelerPhoto.com*

CLEMMENSEN / GERDTS AND MCKINNEY RESIDENCE

Transitional Style

Carol and Larry Clemmensen decided to move from California to Paradise Valley in 2006, and in February 2007, as the residential boom was ending, they purchased a premier lot of just under 5 acres with unobstructed views of Camelback Mountain and its Praying Monk formation.

They asked us to create a two-story home with five en suite bedrooms, a guesthouse, and a four-car garage. In particular, Carol asked for a traditionally styled home inspired by the estates she had experienced in the Hamptons. At the same time, she wanted her home to have a modern, light, and fresh look.

The rear façade combines asymmetrical massing with an axial ground layout. The main doors and windows align with the pool, spa, landscape stairs, and distant peak of Camelback Mountain. *Photo courtesy of Dino Tonn*

The geometry of the living room includes three rectangular double doors, an elevated radiused central window, an interlocked octagonal ceiling, circular porthole windows in quadrants, and walnut flooring set in a chevron pattern. One of the home's many peekaboo balconies connects the first and second levels, while focal-point Camelback Mountain is so prominent it's almost present in the room. *Photo courtesy of Dino Tonn*

Like so many others, the couple put their project on hold at the start of the Great Recession in 2008. However, as the downturn continued, they saw the opportunity to build at a significant discount, and so about eighteen months later, in April 2009, we broke ground. The project bridged our firm's first and second decades, and we were glad to have work when it was scarce.

To accomplish the transitional style Carol described, which was relatively new to our classical-leaning firm, we worked with Scottsdale interior designer Donna Vallone and her team and studied the inspirational images of exteriors and interiors the Clemmensens brought us. Then we edited down the details, incorporated them into our design, and brightened and lightened the palette to create a Hampton manor type of house that retains its timelessness more than a decade later. Our guiding principles are founded on historic architectural styles and mathematic formulas that have been used through the centuries.

A fireplace-warmed sitting vignette of couches and chairs offers the coziness of conversation, and the doors to the backyard invite guests to enjoy the pool, spa, fire pit, and cooking area. The billiards room is just to the right. *Photo courtesy of BradleyWheelerPhoto.com*

Next page: Shadow patterns and reflections animate the natural material palette of stone, glass and steel. *Photo courtesy of Pearl Blossom Photography*

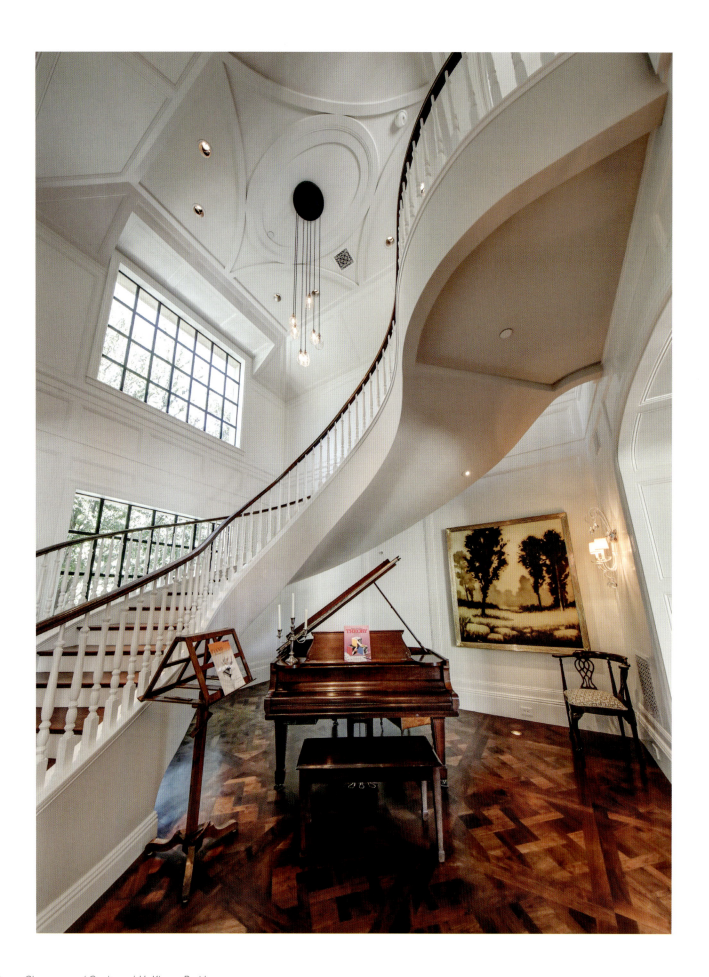

Clemmensen / Gerdts and McKinney Residence

Previous page, left: One of two winding staircases in the home, the grand staircase begins its ascent at the front entry, creating a cozy piano niche beneath. The sinuous staircase mimics the swirling ceiling design and oval pendants centered above. A windowed wall contributes to the light, floating effect. *Photo courtesy of Pearl Blossom Photography*

Previous page, right: Softly lit with LEDs, the cocoon-like parlor invites quiet end-of-day wind-downs. The coffered ceiling and mirroring shelves flanking the fireplace provide a strong geometric theme, a characteristic of Candelaria-designed homes. *Photo courtesy of Dino Tonn*

In contrast to the light-filled living room, the adjacent billiards room is subdued and nostalgic with its tin ceiling, wood wainscoting, low wood table, tall pool chair, triple pendant lighting, and walnut floors. At left is a small bar with a retro-style arch. *Photo courtesy of BradleyWheelerPhoto.com*

Candelaria homes are typically designed around one or more axis points that determine siting and structure and emphasize formal geometry. Here, the landmark mountain to the southwest immediately set that focal point. Organizing the house around that view meant shifting its position on the corner lot. Rather than place it square with the street grid, we twisted the home on the diagonal so that its longest dimension faces the view of Camelback Mountain.

The foyer immediately communicates the home's spaciousness and flow. To the left of the entry is one of the home's two helix staircases, where two-story windows illuminate the ascent to the bedrooms. To the right is a cozy parlor with teal-colored panels reminiscent of early sitting rooms. Directly ahead of the entry hall, visitors are greeted with a view of the living room, where two-story steel windows and doors celebrate the landmark mountain beyond.

A generous hallway on the cross-axis connects to serene courtyards and garden vignettes. To the right of the living room is the billiard room, whose paneling, tin ceiling, and herringbone floors lend a nostalgic feel. An adjoining exercise room also has views to the backyard.

Outside the family room, landscape designer Jeff Berghoff created a shaded fire pit with crunchy gravel for added texture. Candelaria-designed homes feature numerous vignettes, courtyards, and secluded niches. *Photo courtesy of Pearl Blossom Photography*

The kitchen's wood trusses form an enclosing triangular form above the cooking and eating area. A peekaboo balcony sends breakfast aromas into the second floor, drawing the family to the island breakfast table, whose dark woodwork contrasts with the white cabinetry. *Photo courtesy of Pearl Blossom Photography*

In the mirrored and paneled dining room, a large chandelier, dropping from a soffited ceiling, matches the shape and glamour of the wall tilework. This room for formal entertaining conveniently connects to the wine room. *Photo courtesy of Dino Tonn*

Against a wood-plank ceiling, the arching trusswork in the family room matches that in the kitchen. One of the home's many fireplaces offers warmth for small gatherings, and floor-to-ceiling doors and windows draw the eye outside. *Photo courtesy of Pearl Blossom Photography*

Moving around to the south, the kitchen, breakfast room, family room, dining room, wine tower, and study open to gardens, while a second spiral staircase rises to the children's rooms. Above the living room and kitchen are second-floor peekaboo balconies that open in the massing of the two levels and bring natural light to the main level from rooftop dormers.

Beyond the patio, a long, rectangular pool lies on axis with the front door on one end and the mountain peak on the other. Interiors take in views of a formal English-style garden by landscape designer Jeff Berghoff. Flanking the pool on the north-south cross-axis are a cabana and a guesthouse finished in a style reminiscent of 1920s West Hollywood bungalows, including narrow-plank hardwood floors and vintage-inspired appliances and light switches. We choreographed all of the elements to optimize the sight line to Camelback Mountain in one direction, while framing views of the back of the home from the garden.

On the second level is the owners' bedroom suite, where a radiused sitting area mirrors the reading room (the new owners call it the Zen den) on the opposite side of the house. Both of these generously lighted spaces provide emotional centering with Camelback Mountain views. The owners' bath evokes a Hollywood Moderne / Art Deco sense of glamour with its shapes, chandeliers, pewter free-standing tub, millwork, and hardware.

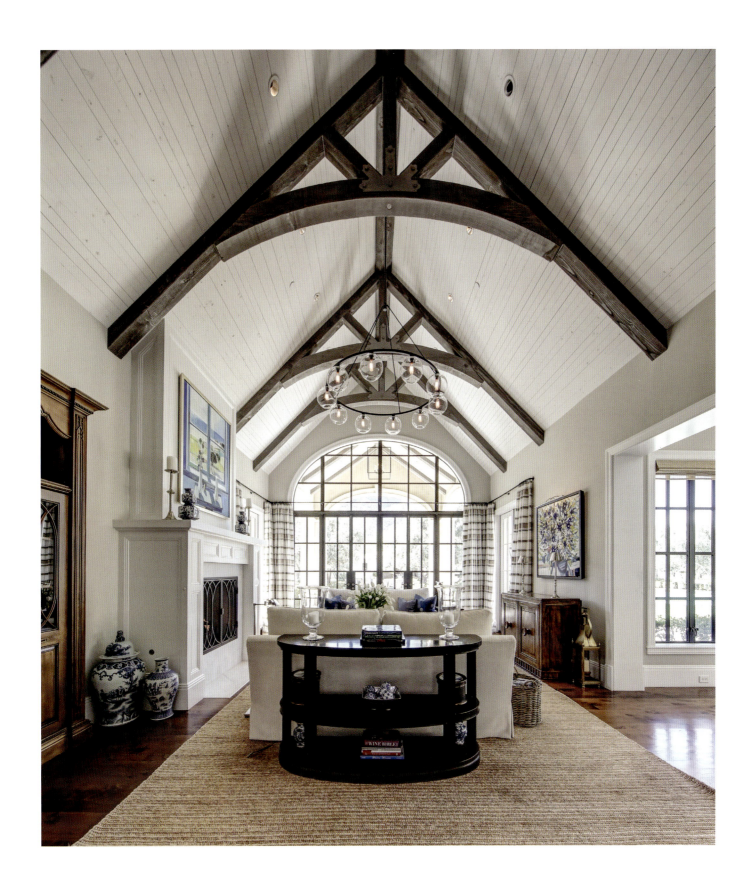

An archway in the primary bath frames a luxurious bathtub, lit by a dripping chandelier. Electronic shades control light and privacy. *Photo courtesy of Pearl Blossom Photography*

A radiused shaped sitting area in the owner's suite provides relaxation and mountain views and acts as a foreground space to the main bedroom area. *Photo courtesy of Pearl Blossom Photography*

The Clemmensens lived there for nearly ten years before selling the home to our former clients in Paradise Valley, Mary Gerdts and Douglas McKinney. Recently, Mary and Douglas asked us to add a detached art studio, an entertainment pavilion, a caretaker's cottage featuring a turreted office matching the style of the main house wine cellar, and six garage bays. They are redecorating with French furnishings and artworks and adding more landscaping, including perimeter oak trees. This residence has hosted extravagant fashion shows, simple barbecues, and, most recently, a "Chakra-tini" party featuring a unique martini for each of the body's seven chakras. Other clients with whom we are working regularly ask to visit. Elegant and expansive without sacrificing warmth, it conveys "home."

The upstairs reading room, with diagonally set book niches near the windows, is everyone's favorite space. The owners call it the Zen den. *Photo courtesy of Dino Tonn*

Next page: Pool, spa, and garden vignettes offer views of the home in one direction and Camelback Mountain in the other. To the left is the detached guesthouse; to the right is the fire pit. *Photo courtesy of BradleyWheelerPhoto.com*

HALIBUT PUTTANESCA

This is a favorite seafood dish that I love to make for pescatarian clients and friends, such as Carol Clemmensen.

SERVES 4

INGREDIENTS

olive oil and a tablespoon or 2 of butter

4 to 6 4-inch-square halibut fillets—skin on or off

½ onion chopped or 2 chopped shallots

6 cloves garlic, diced

1 teaspoon or a dash of red chili pepper flakes

2–3 slices of prosciutto, diced (eliminate for pescatarians)

1 pint of cherry tomatoes, sliced lengthwise, or as many as you want to fill your pan

⅓ cup dry white wine

⅓ cup Kalamata olives

⅓ cup rinsed capers

¼ cup fresh-squeezed lemon juice

zest of ½ a lemon

kosher salt and finely ground fresh pepper

1 teaspoon fresh chopped thyme

1 tablespoon chopped fresh Italian parsley

lemon wedge for garnish

PREPARATION

1. Dry filets and salt and pepper all sides.

2. In a high-sided saucepan set over medium-high heat, warm the olive oil and butter. Brown the fish on both sides for about 2 minutes so it has a nice golden color. Remove from the pan, set on a clean plate, and cover with foil to keep warm.

3. In the same skillet, add the onion or shallots and the garlic and cook until translucent and soft. Sprinkle in the red chile flakes.

4. Add the prosciutto, if desired, and let this cook and crisp up slightly.

5. Toss in the cherry tomatoes and white wine and let the tomatoes cook and soften 7–10 minutes.

6. Add the Kalamata olives, capers, and lemon juice along with the lemon zest, and salt and pepper to taste. Cook this all down into a nice sauce.

7. Let this simmer and thicken up and then nestle the halibut fillets back in, adding some of the tomato sauce over the top of the fish so it is covered.

8. Cook the fish about 5 minutes, covered, so the fish steams. Serve immediately and garnish with the chopped Italian parsley, sprinkles of red chili pepper flakes, and a lemon wedge. Serve over homemade pasta (see "Silverleaf Estate" chapter).

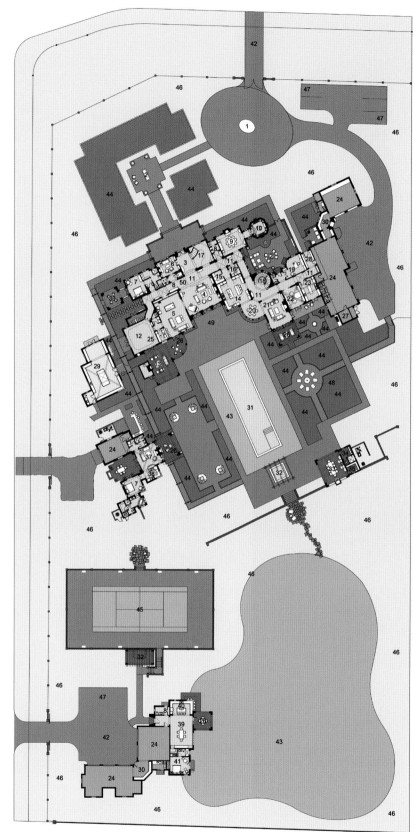

FIRST FLOOR

1. Guest arrival
2. Courtyard
3. Foyer
4. Living room
5. Billiard room
6. Parlor
7. Guest quarters
8. Powder room
9. Dining room
10. Wine room
11. Gallery
12. Exercise room
13. North loggia
14. Kitchen
15. Pantry
16. Butler's pantry
17. Main stairs
18. Back stairs
19. Office
20. Breakfast nook
21. Family room
22. Study
23. Laundry
24. Garage
25. Bar
26. Covered patio
27. Room control
28. Mudroom
29. Art room
30. Workshop
31. Pool
32. Ramada
33. Outdoor kitchen
34. Pool bath
35. Storage
36. Pavilion
37. Guest living
38. Guest kitchen
39. Caretaker living
40. Caretaker kitchen
41. Caretaker quarters
42. Driveway
43. Lawn
44. Garden
45. Tennis court
46. Landscaped area
47. Guest parking
48. Fire pit
49. Grand terrace
50. Elevator

Clemmensen / Gerdts and McKinney Residence • Floor Plan

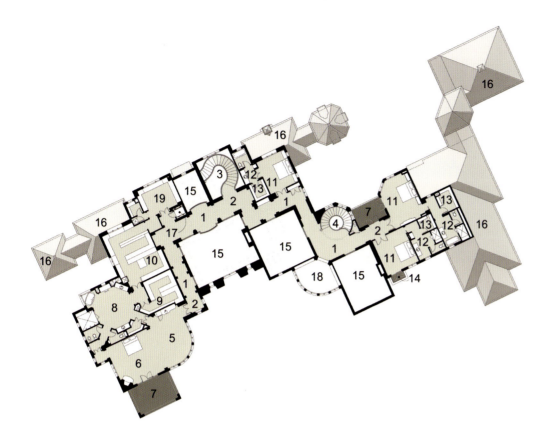

SECOND FLOOR

1. Gallery
2. Vestibule
3. Main stairs
4. Back stairs
5. Primary bedroom sitting room
6. Primary bedroom
7. Terrace
8. Primary bathroom
9. Primary closet
10. Primary closet
11. Secondary bedroom
12. Bathroom
13. Closet
14. Balcony
15. Open to below
16. Roof below
17. Elevator
18. Reading room
19. Office

Mark's original Clemmensen rendering shows Camelback Mountain peeking above the home and anticipates a lush front yard that guides visitors to the front door. The European-inspired home extends east and west on almost 5 acres.

MESSMER RESIDENCE

Santa Barbara at Mummy Mountain

As 2010 progressed, the Great Recession continued its assault on the Phoenix metro area real-estate market and our eleven-year-old firm. Those who were able to withstand this knew, however, that they could build homes at reduced costs, with land and labor prices collapsing 30–50 percent from the boom levels of a few years before.

Fortunately for us, several small on-hold remodels were reactivated and new projects appeared. Phoenix-area luxury builder and good friend John Schultz called. One of his clients had just purchased 2.86 acres on a quiet Paradise Valley street a half mile north of landmark Mummy Mountain. We had already designed two homes to the west and six to the east.

Previous page, left: As shown on the rear façade, the home's tile roofs, Spanish-style chimney, and ironwork detailing evoke Santa Barbara architecture. *Photo courtesy of Werner Segarra*

Previous page, right: The sprawling footprint defines multiple areas for outdoor enjoyment: lawns and ornamental gardens, courtyards, a sports court, a large vegetable garden, and a pool and pool cabana. *Photo courtesy of Phil Johnson*

A meandering approach to the front door diverts the focus from cars. Visitors walk through the gardens from the street or from the auto court behind a Moorish-inspired archway that also keeps the garage out of sight. *Photo courtesy of Pearl Blossom Photography*

John and I and our firm's lead architect, Jeff Kramer, walked the property with the original owner, who envisioned a two-story home with three en suite bedrooms and a casita. They had a clear idea of what they wanted: a Santa Barbara–style design but with a modernist edge, and our challenge was to seamlessly blend the two.

During our two twenty-plus years in business, we have had requests for many different styles—Italian, Spanish, French, and so on. Our job is to listen and understand their wishes and then deliver a composition that embraces their stylistic goals and also connects with the natural surroundings.

We had just completed the design of another Santa Barbara–inspired home, and a trip to Montecito, the unincorporated community east of Santa Barbara, provided additional inspiration. Santa Barbara homes have characteristic white exteriors, tile roofs, arches, low-pitched gable roofs, courtyards, patios, and extensive windows so residents can enjoy, in this instance, the ocean light. But it can feel too heavy and detailed for some people, our client included. Modern design, by contrast, is crisper, stripped of ornamentation and other style indicators. With that in mind, we carefully selected Spanish and Moorish shapes and details but edited and simplified them.

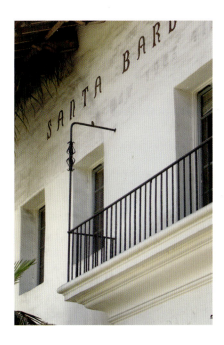

Our visits to classic homes in Santa Barbara influenced the Messmer house details. Shown here are Casa del Herrero, the House of the Blacksmith. It was designed in 1922 by distinguished painter and architect George Washington Smith (1876–1930), who championed Spanish colonial design in Southern California. The style was popularized in Arizona and New Mexico. Regional features of other iconic houses include wrought iron work on balconies and window grilles.

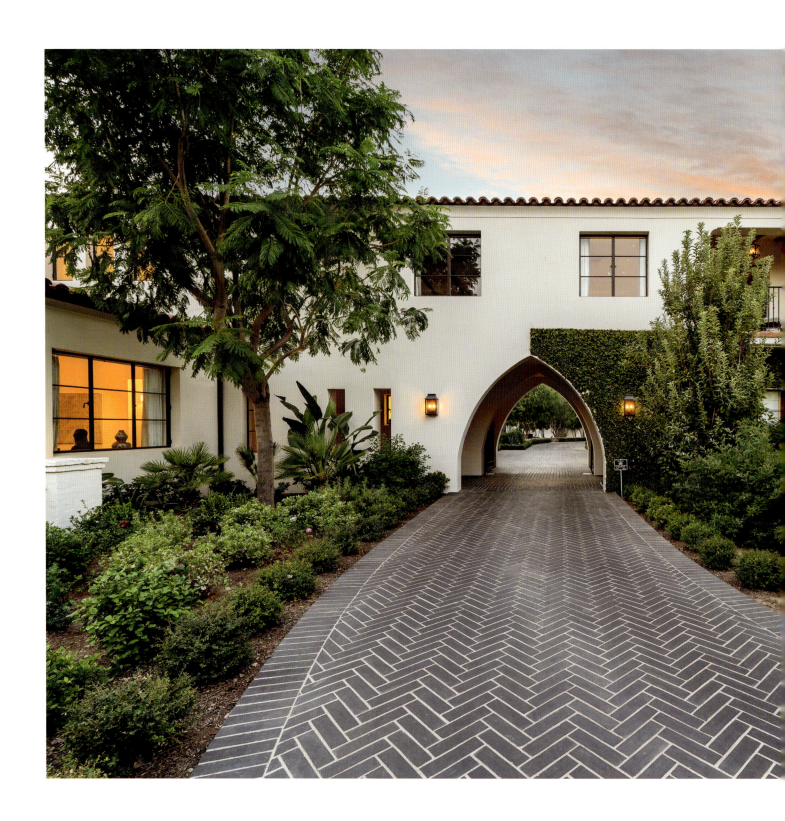

During a second immersive trip to Santa Barbara with John and Jeff, interior designer David Michael Miller, landscape designer Jeff Berghoff, and our client, we continued to study the local architecture and landscaping. We visited some of the homes of architect and painter George Washington Smith (1876–1930), including his 1922 masterpiece, Casa del Herrero (House of the Blacksmith) and its equally inspiring gardens. Both are on the National Register of Historic Places. The influential Smith designed approximately eighty homes in Santa Barbara County. We also visited the Montecito Inn, developed by silent-film legend Charlie Chaplin and his co-investors in 1928. We walked the famous gardens at San Ysidro Ranch and toured the 22-acre Four Seasons Resort, the Biltmore. This Spanish colonial–style hotel most influenced the final design of our client's home, with its auto portal, Moorish-style arches, and other details. At each stop, we noted the buildings' massing, details, plantings, colors, textures, scale, and proportions. Touring and dining together united the group, which is a benefit I came to discover while leading our annual Italy tours. We have since added Spain to our tour itinerary.

Paring down was essential to interpreting the Santa Barbara Modern style our clients had in mind. Low-profile windows and doors and pocketing screens and window walls provide transparency and openness to the outdoors, which is essential to both Santa Barbara and modernist architecture. We realized that only a thin-sash steel window would build this aesthetic bridge our client desired. That led to an international search for the perfect window products—to London, upstate New York, and back to California to visit manufacturers and showrooms. Finally, we selected Riviera Bronze in Ventura for its superior craftsmanship.

At the front of the house, an arching portal leads to the auto court and garages. The team was inspired by the world-famous Four Seasons Hotel in Santa Barbara, where a curving entry drive leads to the front door and an adjacent wing containing a pass-through portal. *Photo courtesy of Phil Johnson*

View from the primary suite to the fountain, pool and cabana, and Mummy Mountain. *Photo courtesy of Pearl Blossom Photography*

The north-facing foyer provides a bright welcome. The custom entry door, designed by David Michael Miller, combines Spanish colonial wood details with small glass lenses that lend a modernist spin. It was fabricated by Sonoran Doors in Phoenix. The chandelier is by the English company Charles Edwards. *Photo courtesy of Pearl Blossom Photography*

The more streamlined exterior complements David's modern interior treatments. For example, the ultramodern Bulthaup kitchen includes solid white oak doors, and the island is an extended brushed stainless-steel cube the company calls "monoblock." In addition, slim, bifolding steel windows connect the room with the outdoors, a signature of the Arizona lifestyle.

We always factor in the views and, whenever possible, place the home on axis with a topographical landmark. Here the corner home is positioned at a slight angle to maximize the view of Mummy Mountain to the south. The landscaping provides changing vignettes, with intimate gardens opening to expanses of lawn.

Owned today by California natives Matt and Brittany Messmer, this home represents one of the first projects in which we started with a classical style and merged it with another. And, as always, the project was as much about building a home as it was about building relationships. We associate many wonderful memories with this home, our inspirational trips, and the team involved in its creation and construction.

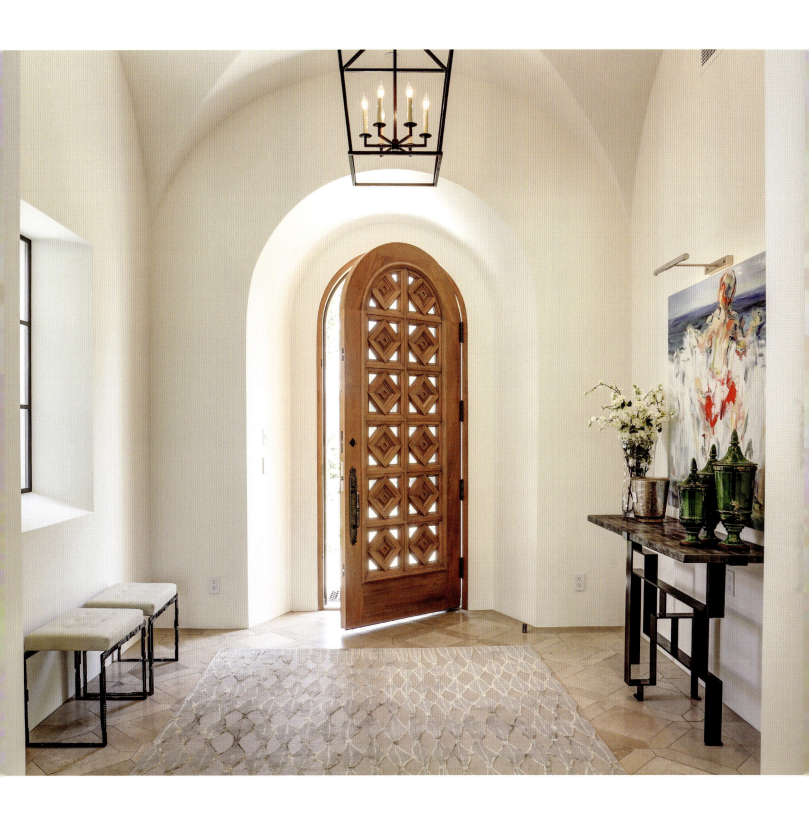

In a clean, earth-toned space, the owners rise and retire to views of Mummy Mountain, whose shape suggests a figure wrapped for eternity. Their bedroom suite also gazes over a water feature, pool, and pool cabana. *Photo courtesy of Phil Johnson*

The sleek Bulthaup kitchen has solid white oak cabinetry doors and a brushed stainless steel "monoblock" island. In this spirit, durable steel thin-sash windows provide transparency here and throughout the home. *Photo courtesy of Werner Segarra*

The home's rear view celebrates the synthesis of architecture and landscape, inspired by a visit to the Four Seasons Resort the Biltmore Santa Barbara. Project architect Jeff Kramer recalled, "We liked the cleanliness, massing, and scale of the hotel exteriors and how the landscaping integrated with the architecture at every turn." *Photo courtesy of Pearl Blossom Photography*

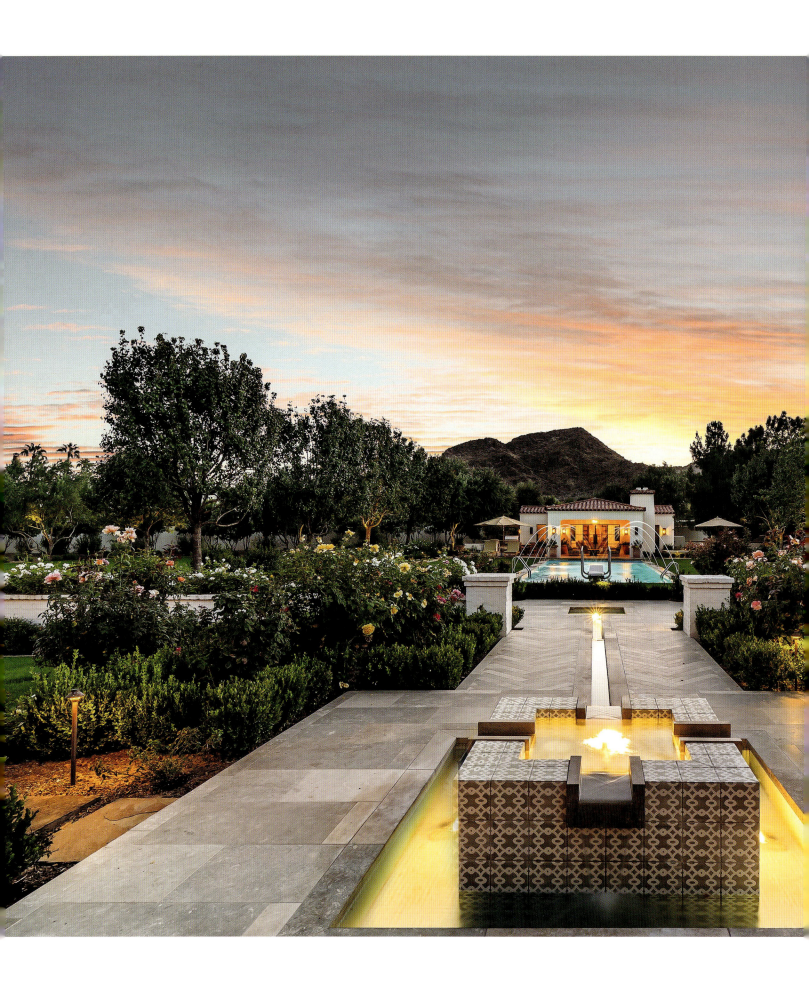

Elevation changes intensify the drama of the Mummy Mountain axis. As if choreographed, a Southwest sunset of orange, teal, and yellow mirrors the cabana lighting. *Photo courtesy of Phil Johnson*

Stairs lead to the children's and nanny's rooms. The custom triptych adds color and delicacy, and the whimsical twisting trees echo the radiused balusters. *Photo courtesy of Pearl Blossom Photography*

GRILLED PEACH, PROSCIUTTO, GOAT CHEESE, AND TRUFFLE HONEY PIZZA

Making pizza is an art form that I admire. There is no one better at it than my friend and amazing James Beard chef Chris Bianco. His passion for pizza inspired me, along with many trips to Italy, where I have often been invited into the kitchen to observe, participate, and learn. The pizza combinations are endless, but this is one of my late-spring, early-summer favorites when peaches come into season.

SERVES 4

INGREDIENTS

Dough

If I'm in a hurry, I will just pick up premade packaged pizza dough in the supermarket. But if I have the time, I stick with Chris Bianco's dough recipe in his book *Bianco: Pizza, Pasta, and Other Food I Like*.

Pizza

⅓ cup flour and a tablespoon of cornmeal for dusting the pizza peel

drizzle of olive oil

5 small semiripe yet firm peaches in season, skin on

2 ounces goat cheese, torn into pieces

2 slices prosciutto, torn into pieces

5 sage leaves, diced

dash of oregano

drizzle of truffle honey

torn fresh basil to garnish

PREPARATION

1. Dust a wood pizza peel with flour and cornmeal.

2. Roll out dough and stretch and pull to desired size and shape.

3. Lay dough out flat and poke the dough with a fork to help distribute the heat while cooking.

4. Drizzle lightly with olive oil.

5. Cut the peaches in half and remove the stem and seed. Brush the peaches with oil and grill lightly enough to produce grill marks. Once they're grilled, slice the peaches into bite-sized, wedge-shaped pieces and distribute them on the pizza.

6. Tear the prosciutto slices into bite-sized pieces and distribute on the pizza. Repeat the same process with the goat cheese.

7. Distribute the diced sage leaves and add a dash of oregano all over the pizza.

8. Slide the pizza from the peel onto a 400°F–600°F pizza stone in your oven or pizza oven. Rotate the pizza as it bakes so that it cooks evenly.

9. Remove from oven, drizzle on the truffle honey, sprinkle with the torn basil, cut, and serve.

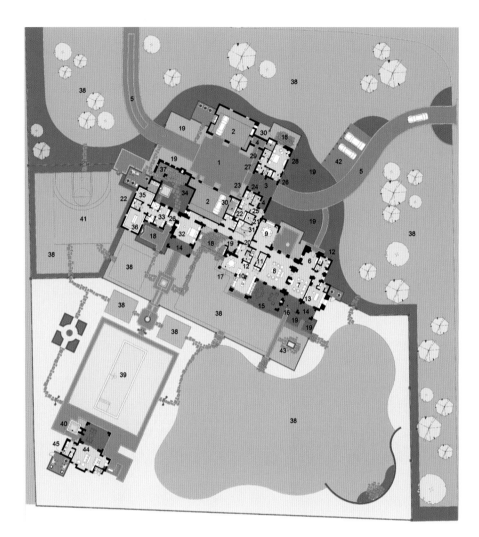

FIRST FLOOR

1	Garage auto court
2	Garage
3	Covered auto portal
4	Covered portal
5	Driveway
6	Foyer
7	Parlor
8	Family room
9	Dining room
10	Kitchen
11	Pantry
12	Powder room
13	Office
14	Covered patio
15	Covered living
16	Trellis patio
17	Breakfast nook
18	Courtyard
19	Garden
20	Command center
21	Wine storage
22	Storage
23	Laundry
24	Dog room
25	Back foyer
26	Vestibule
27	Bath
28	Guest suite
29	Closet
30	Utility room
31	Main stairs
32	Primary bedroom
33	Primary bath
34	Primary suite courtyard
35	Primary closet
36	Primary closet
37	Loggia
38	Landscaped area
39	Pool
40	Spa
41	Basketball court
42	Guest garage
43	Fireplace
44	Pool cabana
45	Pool bath

Messmer Residence • Floor Plan

SECOND FLOOR

1. Main stairs
2. Vestibule
3. Study
4. Bedroom 1
5. Closet
6. Bathroom
7. Bedroom 2
8. Playroom
9. Balcony
10. Laundry
11. Exercise room
12. Outdoor stairs
13. Outdoor deck
14. Covered deck
15. Open to below
16. Roof below
17. Covered balcony

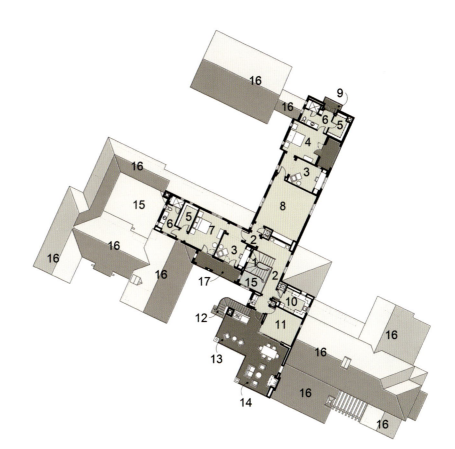

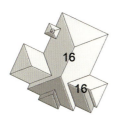

Against a dramatic cloud cover at dusk, the Tuscan farmhouse in North Scottsdale showcases its material richness of fieldstone walls, wood, aluminum, and Jerusalem stone pavers. *Photo courtesy of Pearl Blossom Photography*

SILVERLEAF ESTATE

Tuscan-Inspired Farmhouse in the Scottsdale Foothills

In 2008, the recession was pummeling the Phoenix luxury market, but we could see signs that the market was fighting back. An Ohio couple called to ask if we had designed homes in Silverleaf, now one of North Scottsdale's premier communities. In fact, we had designed the first Silverleaf home in 2002.

The husband mentioned he had heard of our tours to Italy, and, in that spirit, he and his wife wanted to create a Tuscan-inspired home where the family could escape the cold, drab midwestern winters. He asked when the three of us could meet. I remember telling him, "You name it, and I will be there!"

An Umbrian farmhouse we enjoyed on the Candelaria Design Tour Italy provided inspiration for the design.

The fire pit terrace offers spectacular elevated views of a Silverado Golf Course fairway and the McDowell Sonoran Preserve. *Photo courtesy of Pearl Blossom Photography*

Together we walked the golf course lot, defined by lush high desert, an extended knoll along one side of the fairway, and, behind it, the 30,580-acre McDowell Sonoran Preserve, the largest urban preserve in the continental US, with mountain biking and hiking trails the couple planned to enjoy. The three of us discussed the size of the home, the Italian farmhouse style, and the spaces they wanted their home to include.

We soon got right to work with the team: builder Anthony Salcito; interior designer David Michael Miller; landscape designer Jeff Berghoff; and lighting designer Walter Spitz. Looking at the views, we realized that if we raised the finished main floor a few feet, the view really opened up north and east over the knoll to the mountains.

When we staked out the home on the site and simulated the raised floor, we could see just how fantastic the views would be. At the same time, we had to program the excavated space below the main level. Our clients opened up their wish list and added a game room, another bedroom, a full gym and Pilates room, and a twelve-car collector garage just below the five-car family garage on the main level.

The couple admired the community's Italian/Mediterranean-inspired Silverleaf Clubhouse and wanted their home to mirror that style with a mixture of mortar-washed stone, brick, stucco, clay tile roofs, focal-point courtyards, and sand-colored plaster on the interior. We shared photos from our many travels to Umbria and Tuscany and imagery from the books on our shelves. After developing a list of spaces, our team started the design.

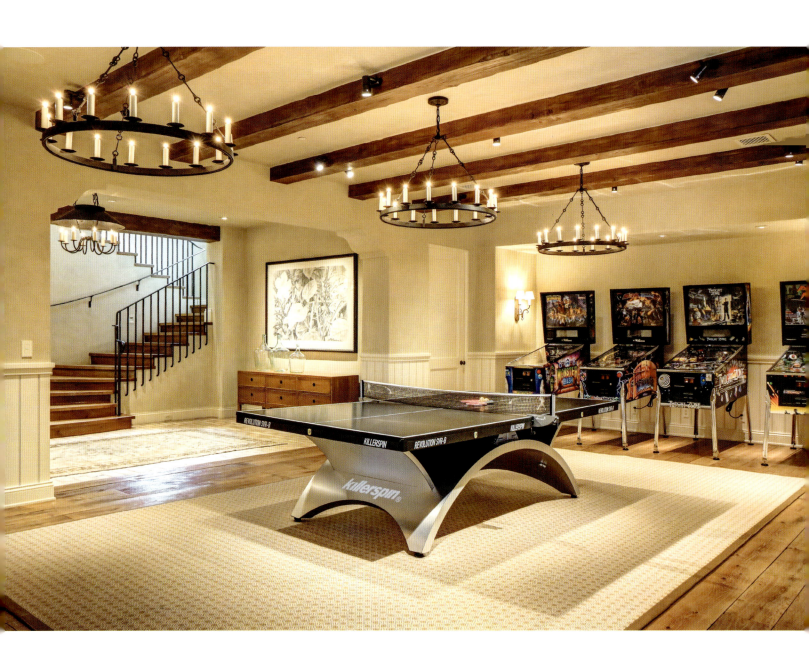

David Michael Miller finished the lower-level game room in neutral tones. A trio of wagon-wheel chandeliers and a custom rug by Miller are among the other design elements. *Photo courtesy of Pearl Blossom Photography*

The gym contains a full Pilates studio and space for the owner's car collection. Salcito Custom Homes excavated this level from the rocky site. *Photo courtesy of Pearl Blossom Photography*

The concept elevation incorporated elements from the clients' wish list and their ideas from a design charrette in which they arranged the various spaces on a site map.

After making a freehand sketch of a home's footprint, our team cuts out pieces of cardboard that correspond to the clients' requests for room sizes and uses and views. Together with the owners, we puzzle them out on a site map until all the pieces make a satisfying composition.

The design concept takes its cues from Italian hill-town homes with rambling masses and rooflines creating engaging courtyards, and in this case capturing views of the Silverleaf course and the McDowell Mountains beyond.

As part of our design process, we make cutouts of the rooms that clients request and then collaboratively place these on a site plan that shows the topography—here the golf course, knoll, foothills, and mountains. This allows us to evaluate hundreds of options with our clients. The process forces us to listen, and it allows the clients to be involved in their design. We want our clients to have the home they want, not the one we want for them.

One of our favorite elements to design are ceilings that complement the spaces below. In this home, we designed meticulously crafted groin vaults, timber trussing, and, in the kitchen, a focal-point brick barrel-vault cupola.

David's work on the interiors achieved the client's desired balance between the heavier Tuscan rural Mediterranean style and the restrained modern style in which he specializes. The spaces are sophisticated yet comfortable and, unlike many Tuscan-inspired homes, light and airy. He chose a light color palette and refined textures on the interior, while we maintained the traditional Italian farmhouse materials and details on the exterior. On the lower level, the wife particularly enjoys the family-memory corridor, with artwork painted by her adult sons when they were boys, all elegantly framed by David.

The pool cabana was inspired by an Umbria farmhouse porch we visited in Italy. It's one of many locations on the property in which to gather and enjoy the high-desert views. *Photo courtesy of Pearl Blossom Photography*

Next page: The house was elevated on the site to capture longer views from the grounds and interiors. *Photo courtesy of Pearl Blossom Photography*

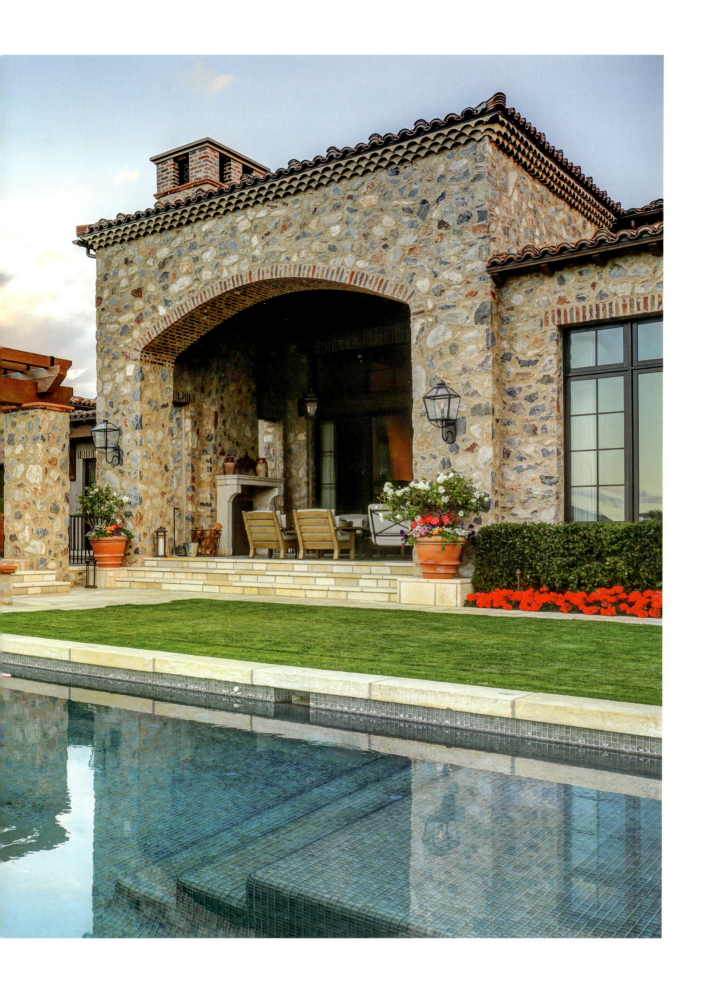

In the family room, exposed Douglas fir trusses and twin iron chandeliers strengthen the farmhouse spirit. *Photo courtesy of Pearl Blossom Photography*

The kitchen's domed brick ceiling admits natural daylight and celebrates the core of the home, where the wife loves to cook and family and friends gather. A double-level chandelier in the cupola illuminates the marble countertops and solid French oak floors. *Photo courtesy of Pearl Blossom Photography*

Naturally lit by glass doors and transoms, the dining room reaffirms the house's earthy color palette with integrally colored plaster walls. The furnishings are more formal than in other spaces. *Photo courtesy of Pearl Blossom Photography*

Dining-room concept sketch by Mark Candelaria

Interior designer David Michael Miller and Mark prepare to board the client's private jet for a quick trip from Scottsdale to Los Angeles to source materials at Exquisite Surfaces, including white oak floors, hammered-limestone floors, fireplaces, tile, and reclaimed items.

One of several Italian-inspired courtyards, this one outside the owner's suite focuses on a spigot water feature. The shady space and sound of water provide a sense of serenity. *Photo courtesy of Pearl Blossom Photography*

Outside, Jeff Berghoff designed gardens that complement the home's interiors. At the entry, low walls and cobbles from Belgium center on an old ironwood tree, which has resplendent lavender blossoms in spring. From here a walkway between green lawns offers an oasis-like approach.

Variously crafted courtyards, some echoing with the splash of water features, merge with the interiors. Next to the owners' bedroom is the wife's Zen space, with a view to a water fountain through multiple arches.

Almost always, our client collaborations result in long-term relationships, and that was true for this project. One Christmas Eve, we needed to fly to Coeur d'Alene, Idaho, to join the rest of the family but couldn't get a flight because of stormy weather. "Let me take you up there," the husband offered. We met him at Scottsdale Airport on Christmas Eve and boarded his jet, and he dropped us off at the Spokane Airport in the middle of a blizzard. About fifty minutes later by car, our holiday wishes were answered; we were all together in time for Christmas.

A nook in the owner's suite supplies an inviting spot for reading. *Photo courtesy of Pearl Blossom Photography*

HOMEMADE PASTA

I learned to make pasta from my good friend Elizabeth Wholey, who taught cooking classes during our Italy tours. Homemade pasta is the perfect dish to pair with this Tuscan-inspired estate and the homeowners' large family. Once you've tasted fresh pasta, there is no comparison to store-bought, and the more times you make it, the easier it gets.

SERVES 8

INGREDIENTS

4½ cups flour

6 eggs

PREPARATION

1. The ingredients are simple: flour and eggs. The quantity of flour to eggs will be adjusted as you go, so you must mix the pasta by hand. The idea is to create a dough that doesn't stick to your hands or the board you're working on. If it's too dry, add another egg; if it's too wet, add more flour.

2. Always dust your pasta board and your hands with flour so the dough does not stick to them. You will use this technique all the way through the process. Fill a large pot at least 5 inches deep with water. Cover and put on the stove to boil; add one heaping tablespoon of coarse salt.

3. To make the pasta, start out with 4½ cups of flour and six eggs. On a large, flat board, pour out the flour and shape into a mound. Make a valley in the middle of the mound; create a volcano! Break the eggs into the volcano and beat them with a fork. With a fork, begin to cover the eggs with flour and continue little by little, mixing in just enough flour so that the dough eventually sticks together uniformly. Or you can cheat and make the mixture in your electric mixer!

4. Flour your hands and knead the dough for 8 minutes until it is shiny and elastic. To test its readiness, stick your finger into the middle of the dough. If it comes out clean, the dough is ready for the pasta machine. If the dough is still sticky, knead in a little more flour.

5. *Important:* Let the dough rest for 10–20 minutes. It can also be wrapped tightly and refrigerated at this point, to be rolled out the next day.

6. Cut the dough ball into quarters or slices, which are easy to roll. Start with the pasta machine dial on 1 and keep rolling the dough through, adjusting the setting higher until you get to the pasta thinness that feels right for whatever you are making.

7. Once the sheets reach your desired thinness, run them through the fettuccine cutter or the spaghetti cutter. Flour the cutters before you use them so the dough does not stick. Do not let the pasta sheets dry before you use the fettuccine or spaghetti cutters. Once the fettuccine or spaghetti strands are cut, swirl them in mounds on a lightly floured tray or pasta drying rack.

8. Drop the pasta into the boiling water. Fresh pasta cooks quickly, in 3–4 minutes. Don't overcook—you want the pasta to be firm but cooked—al dente. Drizzle with olive oil or butter and grate some Parmigiano-Reggiano cheese over the top, and you have the basics. From there you can endlessly add and explore. There is nothing like fresh, homemade pasta!

Photo courtesy of Pearl Blossom Photography

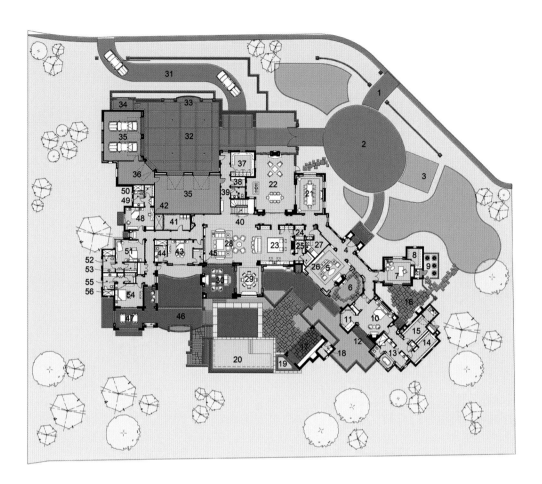

FIRST FLOOR

1	Guest arrival	20	Pool	39	Powder room
2	Guest auto court	21	Dining room	40	Stairs to basement
3	Guest parking	22	Dining courtyard	41	AV storage
4	Entry	23	Kitchen	42	Mechanical chase
5	Living room	24	Butler's pantry	43	Bedroom 1
6	Living courtyard	25	Pantry 1	44	Bathroom 1
7	Office	26	Pantry 2	45	Closet 1
8	Office closet	27	Utility room	46	Trellised bridge
9	Mech yard	28	Great room	47	Covered patio 2
10	Primary bedroom	29	Breakfast nook	48	Bedroom 2
11	Primary bedroom alcove	30	Covered patio 1	49	Bathroom 2
12	Primary bedroom porch	31	Private driveway	50	Closet 2
13	Primary bath	32	Private auto court	51	Bedroom 3
14	Primary closet	33	Balcony	52	Bathroom 3
15	Primary closet	34	Trash area	53	Closet 3
16	Primary bedroom courtyard	35	Garage	54	Bedroom 4
17	Ramada	36	Bike storage	55	Bathroom 4
18	Pool bath	37	Laundry	56	Closet 4
19	Spa	38	Mudroom		

Silverleaf Estate • Floor Plan

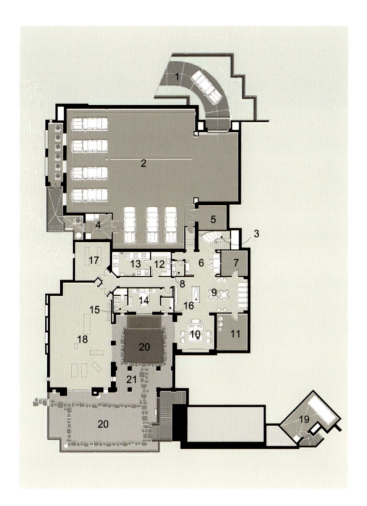

LOWER LEVEL

1. Private auto court
2. Garage
3. Stairs to upper level
4. Garage storage 1
5. Garage storage 2
6. Vestibule
7. Storage
8. Powder room
9. Game room
10. Den
11. Mechanical storage
12. Laundry
13. Mech/utility room
14. Bedroom 5
15. Bathroom 5
16. Closet 5
17. Pilates room
18. Exercise room
19. Pool vault / mechanical room
20. Courtyard
21. Trellised bridge above

A colored concept elevation shows a more detailed vision of the style of the home and materials to be used. This artistic rendering is presented to the homeowners for their approval before building plans are prepared. The design and construction of this foothills home took five years.

A backyard moat protects the owners' cats from bobcats, coyotes, javelinas, and mountain lions. The fire pit seems to float in the moat, which is also safe for swimming. *Photo courtesy of Pearl Blossom Photography*

ITALIAN-MEDITERRANEAN VILLA

A Repository for Art

Just as winter arrived in 2008, we received a call from a representative for clients who were splitting their time between Chicago and Scottsdale. They had purchased a 5.4-acre estate lot in Silverleaf, a golf community adjacent to the McDowell Mountains of North Scottsdale. The couple liked the community because of its proximity to central Scottsdale and the amenities of the Silverleaf Club and Spa.

We prepared by visiting the site and eliciting as much information from their rep as we could. They would be interviewing several architects, and, given the troubled economy, we really wanted this project. We were pleased to get their nod.

At our Phoenix office, the clients shared their vision for an elegant two-story home that was cat friendly—perhaps the first such brief we had encountered! We teamed up with interior designer Kimberly Colletti, lighting designer Walter Spitz, and landscape designer Jeff Berghoff, all in Scottsdale. As they had done with architects, the owners vetted multiple builders and chose Scottsdale's John Schultz.

Their lot slopes southwest toward a fairway of the Silverleaf Golf Course, which undulates with the desert foothills. In the distance are lower elevations, mountains, and city lights; behind the home is a saddle between two peaks, vibrant with Sonoran Desert signature saguaro cactus. Comprising almost 20,000 square feet on a convenient single level, the masonry home extends 100 yards north to south to accommodate long hallways for the owners' collection of paintings and sculptures.

Then we discussed what a cat-friendly house should look like. The clients wanted to make sure that coyotes, bobcats, and javelina could not access the backyard. We boldly suggested raising the pad of the home to create a moat around an elevated backyard that would keep the wildlife at bay. As we soon discovered, this meant that a two-story home would exceed the allowable height limit, so we developed a single-level design. This turned out to be ideal for our clients because it allows them to age comfortably in place.

The main axis aligns with the slope above the golf course, highlighting the panoramic views. In response, a cross-axis organizes all areas of the home, including the long art corridors. The entry gallery, for example,

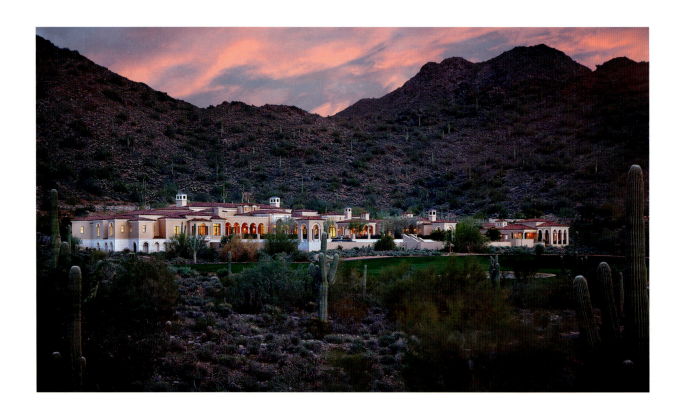

directs you inside and then to the back of the home, where the reflecting pool is on axis with the view south toward the city. The negative edge of the swimming pool empties into the encircling cat moat.

Everything from the interiors to the gardens had to express the clients' desire for elegance, formality, and meticulous detail. The library has walnut floors, bookcases milled with clear-select alder, a four-hundred-year-old painting the husband found in Santa Fe, and a Kashmir-sourced wool rug that was two years in the making. Located in the front of the house off the main gallery, this room connects to a quiet courtyard flanked by an office for each spouse.
On the far north wing of the estate, the owners' suite leads to an exercise room; guests can also use the space via a separate entry.

Designed to support various entertaining scenarios, the kitchen is supported by a back prep kitchen with a walk-in refrigerator and an outdoor barbecue area. The guest quarters, a detached guesthouse, and a six-car garage occupy the far south end of the home.

Exceeding the length of a football field, the house was placed to avoid disturbing the saguaro-covered saddle of the McDowell Mountains. The rear of the all-masonry home is adjacent to a hole of the Silverleaf Golf Course. *Photo courtesy of Werner Segarra*

Because the home is sited in the desert foothills, approximately 1,000 feet higher than most of the lower valley, the views extend beyond the adjacent golf course south to Mummy, Camelback, and Piestewa Mountains and, in the distance, South Mountain. *Photo courtesy of Werner Segarra*

Mark sketches this formal house, which features a classically inspired pediment, doorway arch window, embedded columns, and fountain.

 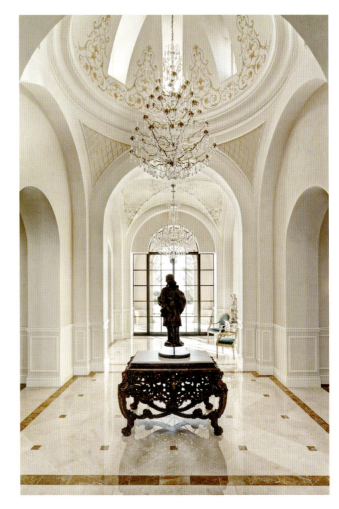

The owners' extensive collection of paintings and sculptures is on display in a light-filled gallery running nearly the length of the house. Inspired by a sculpture at Versailles, interior designer Kimberly Colletti designed the hand-carved marble statue of a woman with a cornucopia in her hand and a lion at her side. *Photo courtesy of Werner Segarra*

The entry gallery leads to the home's main cross-axis. The seventeenth-century Venetian hand-carved *St. Michael* statue is on an Italian table called *The Four Seasons*. Created in 1850, it was carved from a single piece of wood. "It sets the tone for what unfolds in terms of history, quality, and attention to detail," Kimberly says. *Photo courtesy of Werner Segarra*

The grand library is the home's focal point. Finishes and art include select-alder cabinetry, an embellished ceiling, twin chandeliers, walnut floors, a Kashmir rug, possibly one of the oldest paintings made in the United States, and busts of Adam Smith and John Maynard Keynes—which has special meaning for the husband, a retired economics professor. *Photo courtesy of Werner Segarra*

Matching the style of the library, this is one of two adjoining offices. One of the two offices flanking the library has a coffered ceiling and three sets of windows providing abundant light. "The home is the epitome of classical elegance, and yet we were able to make it truly livable as well," Colletti says. *Photo courtesy of Werner Segarra*

Viewed from several rooms, the cat courtyard is an oasis for the homeowners' cherished felines. This diversely landscaped pet paradise includes wisteria and star jasmine. One of the workers even painted mice on a wall. *Photo courtesy of Pearl Blossom Photography*

The loggia enjoys views of the fountain, trees, arched moat pavilions, and mountains beyond. *Photo courtesy of Werner Segarra*

The cats are well taken care of, too. From an indoor cat room containing their litter boxes, a cat door leads to their own outdoor oasis, which includes a linear fountain and garden, all covered by a screened trellis to rebuff hawks, owls, and other wildlife.

A glass breezeway separates this feline nook from the rear loggia that runs nearly the length of the home. This allows the rooms adjoining it to connect with the garden, a setup inspired by many joyous dinners at the seventeenth-century Villa San Michele in Florence during our Candelaria Italy tours. Centering the colorful, multitextured landscape is a plinth we designed that holds full-size sculptures of two hunting lionesses designed by Bart Walter of Westminster, Maryland.

The exquisitely crafted home—the most articulated residence we have done—contains many one-off components such as the cabinetry, fireplaces, and limestone carvings. The walls are hand-plastered, and much of the flooring is marble. These polished finishes complement the couple's artworks, along with custom lighting.

Reminiscent of an emperor's villa with its columns and vaults, the loggia was inspired by visits to Villa San Michele, the hilltop hotel in Florence set in a fifteenth-century monastery. *Photo courtesy of Werner Segarra*

Kimberly Colletti's kitchen design features an island with scrollwork corbels, twin chandeliers, and niches with embedded columns holding classical figures. The arched opening leads to the butler's pantry, with a service window to the outdoor kitchen. *Photo courtesy of Werner Segarra*

The dining room incorporates custom millwork and a hand-carved limestone fireplace. The interior design mixes classical architectural details with a glass-topped dining table and modern statuary in the niche. *Photo courtesy of Werner Segarra*

With matching Ionic columns at the soaking tub, her bath features custom millwork, stonework, and marble floors. Custom draperies continue the earth-tone theme, while adding blue-green highlights and delicate tassels. *Photo courtesy of Werner Segarra*

Mark in the grand library

A stone fountain underscores the architectural themes of the front façade. From this turnaround, cars can be parked in one of three garages. *Photo courtesy of Pearl Blossom Photography*

BRAISED SHORT RIBS

This recipe is a family favorite. I've been perfecting it for years, but thanks to the modern pressure cooker, I've recently adapted this recipe to be made in half the time! Here we have an absolutely delicious dish for four that I serve with polenta, risotto, or mashed potatoes. What else but short ribs for a couple with roots in Chicago, the "meatpacking capital of the world"!

SERVES 4

INGREDIENTS

6 pounds or about 8 short ribs

salt and pepper to season generously

2 tablespoons olive oil

1 medium onion, diced

1 tablespoon paprika

1 teaspoon cayenne pepper, or 2 teaspoons if you prefer it spicier

3 tablespoons brown sugar

3 tablespoons balsamic vinegar

6 cloves garlic

2–3 fresh thyme sprigs

1 cup beef stock

½ cup red wine or bourbon

1 pound sliced mushrooms, optional

1 tablespoon cornstarch (corn flour)

1 tablespoon water

Italian or curly parsley for garnish

PREPARATION

1. Fill a large bowl or pot with cold water. Immerse the short ribs and rinse the ribs in the cold water.

2. Drain the short ribs and pat dry with paper towels.

3. Generously sprinkle salt and pepper on all sides.

4. Switch on the Instant Pot to the sauté setting on high.

5. When the Instant Pot is hot, pour in about 2 tablespoons of oil.

6. When the oil is hot, place 3–4 short ribs in the Instant Pot to sear. It's important not to crowd the bottom in order to get nice caramelization on your short ribs.

7. Sear the short ribs on all sides, about 2–3 minutes per side. Place the caramelized short ribs on a plate and cover with foil.

8. Repeat with the rest of the short ribs.

9. Discard excess oil, leaving 1 tablespoon of oil in the Instant Pot.

10. Add the diced onion and some wine or bourbon to deglaze the bottom of the pot and make sure that all of the caramelized bits on the bottom are mixed with the wine (deglazing is an important step, so don't skip it).

11. Add the paprika, cayenne pepper, sugar, and balsamic vinegar. Then switch off the sauté function on the Instant Pot.

12. Place the short ribs back in the Instant Pot and add the garlic, thyme, and a pinch of salt (how much salt to add at this point depends on how well you seasoned the short ribs earlier. Be careful not to over salt; you can always add more at the end if needed).

13. Add the sliced mushrooms, if using.

14. Pour the stock over the short ribs. Seal the Instant Pot lid. Choose the manual high-pressure function and set it to high. Cook the short ribs for 45 minutes, followed by a 10–15-minute natural release.

15. When done, remove the ribs (and mushrooms) with a slotted spoon, set aside and keep warm. Now with the liquid left in the pot, switch on the sauté function and let the liquid come to a boil and reduce. As it reduces, combine the cornstarch with the water in a small bowl to make a paste, and then slowly whisk the paste into the reducing juice in the Instant Pot and continue whisking to make a gravy.

16. Plate the short ribs and mushrooms over homemade pasta (page 70), risotto (page 224), or mashed potatoes. Drizzle with the gravy and garnish with diced fresh parsley.

The façade concept rendering reveals Italianesque elements such as multiple archways, varying tile roof elements, and campanile-style fireplace chimneys.

Taken close to the home's completion, this aerial view shows the cat moat separating the home from the desert, as well as the rear loggia and the arched towers flanking the moat. Swirling fencing marks the property boundaries without fortressing it. *Photo courtesy of Extreme Aerial Photography*

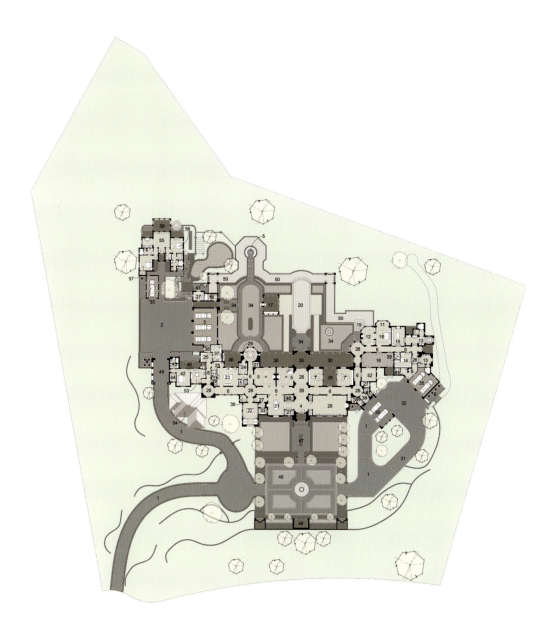

MAIN LEVEL

1. Driveway
2. Guest auto court
3. Guest parking
4. Entry
5. Living room
6. Gallery
7. Office
8. Office closet
9. Mechanical yard
10. Primary bedroom
11. Primary alcove
12. Primary sitting room
13. Primary bath
14. Primary closet
15. Primary closet
16. Primary courtyard
17. Ramada
18. Pool bath
19. Spa
20. Pool
21. Dining room
22. Billiard room
23. Kitchen
24. Butler's pantry
25. Pantry 1
26. Office courtyard
27. Storage
28. Formal library
29. Breakfast nook
30. Loggia
31. Private driveway
32. Private auto court
33. Wine room
34. Garden
35. Garage
36. Grill
37. Laundry
38. Mudroom
39. Powder room
40. AV storage
41. Mechanical room
42. Bedroom 1
42. Bathroom 1
43. Bathroom 1
44. Closet 1
45. Porte cochére
46. Balcony
47. Courtyard
48. Formal auto court
49. Valet
50. Cat moat
51. Fire pit
52. Exercise
53. Bedroom 1 sitting
54. Staff quarters
55. Guest living
56. Guest bedroom 1
57. Guest bedroom 2
58. Guest covered patio

HISTORIC JOHN M. ROSS TUDOR HOME

Escape to the English Countryside

At the start of our firm's second decade, a client asked us to renovate and add to the historic Tudor / Elizabethan Revival John M. Ross Home in north Phoenix, designed in 1929 by Lescher & Mahoney, the city's most-distinguished architecture firm at the time. Our challenges were to fulfill the owners' wish list with sensitivity to its history and to conform to the city's requirements for updating a home approaching its centenary.

As a boy in Phoenix, the new owner had delivered newspapers on his bicycle in the historic Orangewood community of North Central Avenue, the city's defining north-south artery. This address always inspired braking. He admired this prominent piece of architecture on the area's largest residential parcel, 2.89 acres, as well as the gnarly, half-century-old olive trees, expansive lawn, and pasture for sheep, cattle, and horses. When the estate became available in spring 2010, he and his wife snapped it up, becoming the fourth owners.

Previous page: Approaching its centennial, the Tudor / Elizabethan revival home has distinctive red brick with random blackened "klinker" bricks, tufa limestone, a cedar shake roof, and ceramic clay chimney pots. The north entry, formerly a driveway to the front door, now welcomes guests with a walkway among roses and hedges. *Photo courtesy of Dino Tonn*

Wrought iron fencing on the Central Avenue side allows pedestrians a view of the historic home, listed on the National Register of Historic Places. The over-fired klinker bricks can be seen on the gabled entry. *Photo courtesy of Dino Tonn*

"I dreamed about living here, but I never thought it was going to happen," he told me shortly after we met. The exterior looked pretty much the same as the house he remembered, but "the interior was exhausted, a mélange of styles," he said. "In the kitchen, almost nothing had changed since the 1950s." Committed to preserving and living in the historic home, the couple called Phoenix-based Nance Construction, known for fastidious preservations, and the owner, Nancy Brunkhorst, asked us to join the team. Like everyone else, we were limping through the Great Recession, and the competition for commissions was fierce. We were down to nine employees from a high of twenty-six during the housing-market peak in 2008. So, we were thrilled to land this project.

Contractor Hubert R. Meadows built the 4,273-square-foot, two-story main house and adjacent carriage house in the spring and summer of 1929 for attorney John Mason Ross. Characterized by elements such as dormer windows and steeply pitched roofs, Tudor Revival peaked in 1920s Phoenix—1929 in particular—when moneyed residents looked overseas for social distinction and to express nostalgia for preindustrial-age craftsmanship. The brickwork is the home's most prominent structural feature, with randomly placed clinkers. Partly vitrified, blackened, and often misshapen as a result of kiln accidents, these distinctive bricks appear on the main house, the carriage house, and the later-built garage, connecting them stylistically.

The front of the house was almost untouched. Berghoff's encircling pony wall is made from locally quarried DC Ranch field rock. *Photo courtesy of Dino Tonn*

Behind Mark are the original Mr. & Mrs. John Mason Ross building plans prepared in 1928 by Lescher and Mahoney. The owners cherish the blueprints as part of the provenance of the historic home they've admired since childhood. *Photo courtesy of Pearl Blossom Photography*

On axis with a new koi pond on the north and a new pool and pool house to the south, the steel and glass pavilion connects the main house on the left with the garage on the right. *Photos courtesy of Dino Tonn*

An updated landscape honors the original tone of a quiet Tudor home in a country setting. The pond, which uses irrigation water from the canal along Central Avenue, is stocked with live bass and is a perfect spot for a summer dip. *Photo courtesy of Dino Tonn*

On February 24, 2000, the two buildings entered the National Register of Historic Places. Auxiliary structures, such as the four-car garage next to the main house, built in 1975 by the former owners, are considered historically nonconforming. The clients wanted the main house and garage joined for convenience and aesthetics, and the Arizona State Historic Preservation Office required a contrasting connecting structure to mark the two buildings' differing time periods. Our response was to create an almost transparent metal and glass pavilion that links them. The team began its design work in June 2010.

This new pavilion, or conservatory, is aligned with the existing pool and a new pool house behind it. To the west, a new irrigation pond designed by Jeff Berghoff underscores the pastoral theme. He also set a rectangular koi-stocked pond in the front garden. Aligned with the conservatory,

The renovated kitchen includes twin farm sinks and twin ball pendants over the breakfast island, plaster ceiling molding, two three-sided leaded glass cabinets, and a Lacanche double oven/range. Beneath the kitchen, the original basement is now a wine cellar accessed from a trap door. A small office/mudroom lies toward the back. *Photo courtesy of Dino Tonn*

The fifties-vintage kitchen was renovated and expanded with views to the backyard through the breakfast nook. Oak floors, a custom walnut island, and radiused white cabinetry look like they could have been original. *Photo courtesy of Dino Tonn*

The renovated carriage house became a game room, bar, and guesthouse. Exposed Douglas fir truss work is set against the Engelmann spruce wood ceiling. The floor is integrally colored concrete. Visible through the window is the garage, now attached to the main house by means of the pavilion. *Photo courtesy of Dino Tonn*

The attic of the original detached garage was repurposed as a light-suffused exercise room. Large ceiling fixtures and LED lighting provide additional illumination. Windows from the main house can be seen through the background window. *Photo courtesy of Dino Tonn*

the water feature unites the main residence and garage with the carriage house just north. All three buildings connect along intersecting north-south and east-west axes.

After receiving approval from the city and the preservation office, Nance Construction started work on the house in November 2010 and finished in June 2012. It was gutted to the studs and its floor plan reconfigured to accommodate the needs of the owners and their two children.

We shifted the owners' suite and children's bedrooms to create a more orderly flow of rooms. The kitchen received the most dramatic change; it was opened on each side to allow light to flow across the space. To the low ceiling we added an embossed pattern for interest and detail. The hardwood floor and the patinaed zinc hood with brass accents maintain the room's historical connection. In the expanded kitchen, a large window overlooks the lawn, pool, and pond. To maximize space, we

Lit by east-facing windows, the remodeled primary bath has a carved single-slab-marble tub in a field of honed mosaic marble squares. Other details include marble-topped cabinets and vanity, plaster walls and ceiling coving, and a marble steam shower. *Photo courtesy of Dino Tonn*

replaced the original steps to the basement under the kitchen with a pull-up door to the new wine cellar that neatly pockets into the matching oak flooring. Interior designer Donna Vallone repurposed or rehabbed the main house's spaces, such as the second-floor children's rooms.

The house's exterior was essentially maintained in keeping with historic guidelines. The carriage house, which once contained cars and the boiler system, has become the guest cottage, and the former attic of the garage is now an exercise room. To strengthen the English-countryside theme, Jeff repositioned the driveways, planted flower and citrus gardens, added an entry-walk pony wall, and planted dozens of trees.

Now the property and home work together as one. Well-defined gardens combine with beautiful finishes; new doors, windows, and millwork; and curated furnishings, creating this soft, sophisticated residence that celebrates its history and community.

French doors and glass transoms bookend the east (front) and west (back) of the house. The room is clad in an alder coffered ceiling and millwork. *Photo courtesy of Dino Tonn*

A new pool and cabana reinforce the home's axial layout. *Photo courtesy of Dino Tonn*

SOUTHWEST-STYLE BEEF WELLINGTON

What could be a better recipe for a Tudor / Elizabethan Revival home in Arizona than beef Wellington with a spicy Southwest rub? This dish has become a holiday tradition in our family.

SERVES 8

INGREDIENTS

Southwest Rub

2–3 tablespoons olive oil

2 finely chopped shallots

3 finely chopped garlic cloves

1 pound finely ground button mushrooms

2 teaspoons red chile powder

½ teaspoon black pepper

¾ teaspoon salt

¼ cup bourbon

Beef

3–3½ pounds beef tenderloin cut from the thick center part of the tenderloin, trimmed of fat

1 teaspoon red chili powder

½ teaspoon ground cumin

1 teaspoon salt

3 tablespoons avocado oil

¼ cup Dijon mustard

4 ounces thinly sliced prosciutto

3 sheets (15–20 ounces) puff pastry, thawed, but still cold

2 beaten egg yolks combined with 1 tablespoon water

PREPARATION

Southwest Rub

1. In a large sauté pan over moderate heat, add the oil and sauté the shallots and the minced garlic until they are translucent and soft, about 5 minutes.

2. Add the ground mushrooms, chile powder, salt and pepper, and bourbon. Cook until the mushrooms have released their remaining moisture and the mixture has become dry and paste-like, about 10 minutes. Remove from the pan and let cool.

Beef Preparation and Assembly

1. Season the beef with salt, chili powder, and cumin. In a very hot cast-iron pan, sear the beef in avocado oil, browning all sides.

2. Remove the beef and let cool. Brush all sides with the mustard.

3. On a floured surface, roll out one puff pastry sheet slightly to make a rectangle that is about 2–3 inches larger than the width of your beef on each side. Place the other sheet in the refrigerator until needed.

4. Layer the prosciutto on the puff pastry sheet in an area that is the same size as the beef. Top the prosciutto with about ¼ of the mushroom mixture.

5. Place the beef on top of the prosciutto and mushroom mixture and cover the beef with the remaining mushroom mixture. Layer the remaining prosciutto on top of the mushroom mixture so that the beef is completely encased.

6. Roll the puff pastry around the beef and fold up around the sides. Brush the pastry with the egg wash.

7. Place the extra sheet of puff pastry on top of the beef, pressing it around the beef so that it overlaps the bottom sheet that was folded up the sides to encase the beef. Press the two sheets together so they make a tight fit. Roll up the encased beef in plastic wrap and place in the refrigerator for 30 minutes so that it firms up.

8. Place the beef on a well-greased baking sheet. Brush the beef roll with the egg wash. Using the third sheet of puff pastry, make a lattice with a dough cutter and lay it over the entire top side of the beef pastry roll. Brush the top pastry with more egg wash.

9. Bake in a 425°F degree oven for 40 minutes. Remove from the oven and use a meat thermometer to check for an internal temperature of 120°F. If not to temperature, place back in oven and check every 5 minutes until it reaches 120°F.

10. Remove from oven and let it rest for 15 minutes on a wire rack wrapped in foil. Transfer to a serving dish and garnish with roasted vegetables and diced parsley.

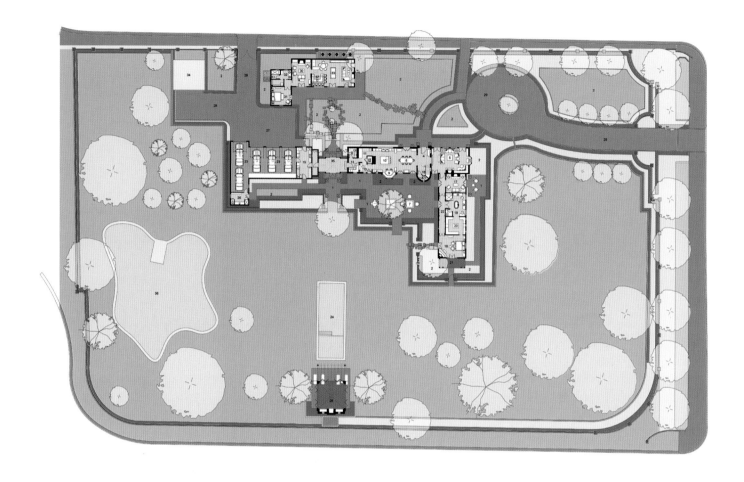

FIRST FLOOR

1 Terrace	14 Auxiliary stairs	27 Motor court
2 Garden	15 Laundry	28 Driveway
3 Lawn	16 Main stairs	29 Guest arrival
4 Foyer	17 Office	30 Guest living
5 Living room	18 Primary bedroom	31 Guest bedroom
6 Dining room	19 Primary bathroom	32 Guest bathroom
7 Fire pit	20 Primary closet	33 Game room
8 Powder room	21 Covered patio	34 Guest parking
9 Breakfast nook	22 Hallway	35 Conservatory
10 Kitchen	23 Garage	36 Pond
11 Back kitchen	24 Pool	37 Bar
12 Walk-in refrigerator	25 Ramada	
13 Room control	26 Pool bath	

104   *Historic John M. Ross Tudor Home • Floor Plan*

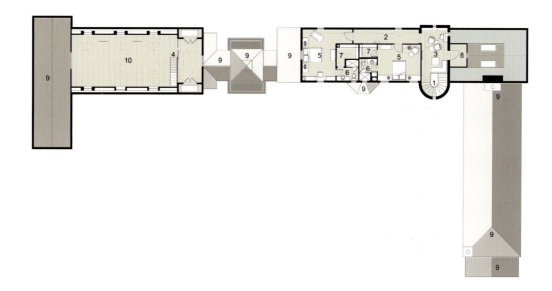

SECOND FLOOR

1. Main stairs
2. Hallway
3. Lounge area
4. Auxiliary stairs
5. Secondary bedroom
6. Bathroom
7. Closet
8. Storage
9. Roof below
10. Exercise room

WYSEL RESIDENCES

Rural Mediterranean in Coastal California

Designing one home for a client is an honor, and doing it a second time is even more rewarding. The two homes we created for Glen and Lisa Wysel, first in Arizona and then in California, were a career highlight. In 2005, the couple asked us to design their Tuscan Mediterranean dream home at the Silverleaf golf course community in North Scottsdale. They were relocating from Santa Barbara and had heard of our work.

The Wysels had toured Italy and wanted their new home to incorporate their memories and passion for Italian architecture. By that time, too, our firm had hosted five tours to Italy and had collected thousands of images of the beautiful countryside and rural architecture of Umbria and Tuscany. We drew on those images and memories in designing the couple's home.

After a two-year design process, Scottsdale builder Ed West began the two-story home in 2008 and completed it two years later. A major goal was to make the most of views of the nearby McDowell Mountains, as well as vistas south through Scottsdale and Phoenix.

Eventually, though, the Wysels missed coastal Montecito, their "favorite place on Earth." In 2012 they retained us to design a retirement home there.

Previous page: The two-story Montecito home fits snugly amid the trees, with the Santa Ynez Mountains in the Los Padres National Forest distant. *Photo courtesy of Bradley Posey*

At the rear, an elevated patio and stepped terraces help ground the building on this small, sloping lot with strict height and setback requirements.

Mark's napkin sketch of the Montecito home, drawn upside-down at a client dinner at a San Ysidoro Ranch restaurant

108 *Wysel Residences*

We encountered several challenges in designing this "second-life" home. One of the last unbuilt parcels in the master-planned Ennisbrook community, the property is smaller than most of the others and has a slightly sloping hillside beginning in the middle of the property and continuing to the rear lot line. This forced us into an even smaller footprint on the flatter, more buildable street-facing side. In addition, the sloping lot made it more difficult to establish sight lines to the Santa Ynez Mountains in the Los Padres National Forest to the north, and to the mature trees near the home. Our solution to both of these issues was to tuck the home into the slope to create a lower level for a two-car garage, freeing up living space on the main level. The second story containing two bedrooms and a lounge has superb views of the Santa Ynez Mountains over a thick canopy of trees.

Completed in 2015, the three-story home has a primary suite on the main floor along with the great room, kitchen, breakfast room, and office. Two additional bedrooms plus a bunk room occupy the upper floor along with three and a half bathrooms. Glen and Lisa wanted spaces that felt cozy, livable, and inviting, with proportions that are not overly grand despite the home's 4,825 square feet.

An aerial view illustrates the three-level "E" shape we used to slot the home into a tight lot among mature trees. *Photo courtesy of Bradley Posey*

The owners' suite is warm and cozy, with light and views to the garden and mountains beyond. The rug was sourced at Azadi Fine Rugs in Scottsdale. *Photo courtesy of Bradley Posey*

The breakfast room has hand-painted tiles in the coffered ceiling, a carved limestone fireplace, and reclaimed wood floors. Just outside, trees and mountains supply privacy and splendor. *Photo courtesy of Bradley Posey*

Next page: The great room's reclaimed ceiling beams and steel doors frame beautiful views of the Santa Ynez Mountains. Furnishings by interior designer Donna Vallone include a custom rug from Azadi Fine Rugs in Scottsdale. "We wanted to go with a neutral palette so the eye would go to the spectacular view outside," she says. *Photo courtesy of Bradley Posey*

Previous page: Donna Vallone and her team designed the front door with an antique look in mind. She sourced the terra-cotta floor tile from Craftsman Court Ceramics in Scottsdale. *Photo courtesy of Bradley Posey*

A wide doorway flanked with matching glass-and-millwork hutches connects the kitchen and breakfast room. Perfect symmetry and axis points guided the composition. *Photo courtesy of Bradley Posey*

The opposing hutches and the island form a soft blue-gray millwork triptych in the kitchen and breakfast room. *Photo courtesy of Bradley Posey*

Every bedroom suite has stellar views of the Santa Ynez mountains on one side and distant views of the Pacific Ocean on the other. The lower level houses a garage and wine cellar, and an elevator connects all three levels. Coffered ceilings and reclaimed wood beams and floors lend a sense of human scale, while steel windows add a refined touch to the rustic, mortar-washed rubble stone and clay tile roofs.

This project is another example of our preference for mixing materials such as wood, stone, steel, and water in our work, whether it is traditional, transitional, or modern. The design process is a lot like cooking, deploying just a few select materials and mixing them in a way that is not overpowering. These materials bring warmth and a connection to the earth in our more modern homes. In our traditional homes we favor a restrained use of both new, found, and reclaimed materials from around the world, using them in unique and creative ways that resonate with our clients.

The first house we designed for the Wysels, in Scottsdale, Arizona, was inspired by rural Italian dwellings, a combination of wood, wrought iron, and stone. Across the pool and fire pit at the rear, views extend for miles to the valley below.

PORCHETTA WITH SALSA VERDE

If you really want to show off your kitchen skills, there is nothing better than making a porchetta on the smoker. It is incredibly delicious, not that difficult, and a great way to serve a large group. I love to accompany this with roasted vegetables.

SERVES 8

INGREDIENTS

Porchetta

6-12 pounds boneless pork belly

½ cup olive oil

kosher salt and pepper to cover the porchetta

½ nutmeg nut, finely grated

2 tablespoons finely powdered fennel seed or fennel pollen powder

2 Honey Crisp apples peeled, cored, and diced

1 red onion, finely chopped

¼ cup finely diced pancetta

¼ cup apple cider vinegar

small handful of basil leaves

small handful of sage leaves

small handful of Italian parsley leaves

¼ cup fresh rosemary

2 tablespoons fresh thyme

fronds of two fennel bulbs

6 garlic cloves, chopped

¼ cup olive oil, or as needed for the herb rub

zest of one orange

zest of one lemon

¼ cup crushed red chile flakes

2 tablespoons kosher salt

2 tablespoons baking soda

Salsa Verde

2 garlic cloves, finely chopped

1 tablespoon capers, rinsed and finely chopped

3-6 anchovies, finely chopped

small handful of basil leaves

small handful of Italian parsley leaves

6 mint leaves

small handful of sage leaves

salt and pepper

1 tablespoon red pepper flakes

juice and finely grated zest of one lemon

olive oil as needed

PORCHETTA PREPARATION

1. Roll out the pork belly and score the meat side with diagonal slits about 1.5 inches apart. Then flip over and score the skin horizontally and vertically about every 2 inches. You might need a sharp utility knife to cut through the tough skin.

2. Flip meat side up and remove about a quarter of the skin from the end of the pork belly where you will begin the rollup. This is optional; it will turn out just fine with all the skin intact.

3. Season the meat side liberally with the salt, pepper, nutmeg, and fennel powder.

4. In a sauté pan, sauté the pancetta, red onion, and apples in about 2 tablespoons of olive oil. As the onions and apples soften, add the apple cider vinegar. Cook until softened and set aside to cool.

5. In a food processor, combine the basil, sage, Italian parsley, rosemary, thyme, fennel fronds, garlic, salt, and pepper. Add a drizzle of olive oil and process until well chopped but not puréed.

6. Now smear this herb paste on the seasoned meat, along with the lemon and orange zest and red chile flakes.

7. Spoon the cooled apples and onions over the first third of the pork belly where you will begin the roll. Keep this layer as thin as possible. If you have extra, don't worry—stop when you've covered a third to half of the pork belly.

Now roll up the pork belly tightly, starting with the end where you removed the skin, if you chose to do so. Once rolled, tie it with butcher twine with 1½-inch spacing so it stays tightly together.

8. Now coat the skin with half of the salt and baking soda mixture. Refrigerate the porchetta overnight or at least 6–8 hours. This will dry out the skin and give it a crunchy texture when roasted.

9. Now to roast! Coat the porchetta with avocado oil, which has a high burn point. Recoat with the remainder of the salt and baking soda mixture. Set on the smoker and let smoke for about two hours.

10. Crank up the heat to 325°F for about an hour, then lower to 225°F for two hours or until the roast's internal temperature reaches 125°F. Then turn up the heat to 450°F to crisp up the skin and bring the internal temperature to 165°F.

11. Remove the porchetta from the grill, tent with foil, and let it rest about 15 minutes.

SALSA VERDE PREPARATION

1. Place all the ingredients in a food processor and process until nearly puréed.

2. Carve the porchetta in half-inch slices and garnish with the salsa verde. Serve with roasted vegetables. The leftovers make an amazing sandwich with the salsa verde and some fresh arugula leaves.

FIRST FLOOR

1. Courtyard
2. Garden
3. Lawn
4. Foyer
5. Great room
6. Dining room
7. Elevator
8. Powder room
9. Studio
10. Kitchen
11. Main stairs
12. Outdoor stairs
13. Laundry
14. Pantry
15. BBQ
16. Covered patio
17. Primary bedroom terrace
18. Primary bedroom
19. Primary bathroom
20. Primary closet
21. Driveway
22. Parking
23. Entry walkway

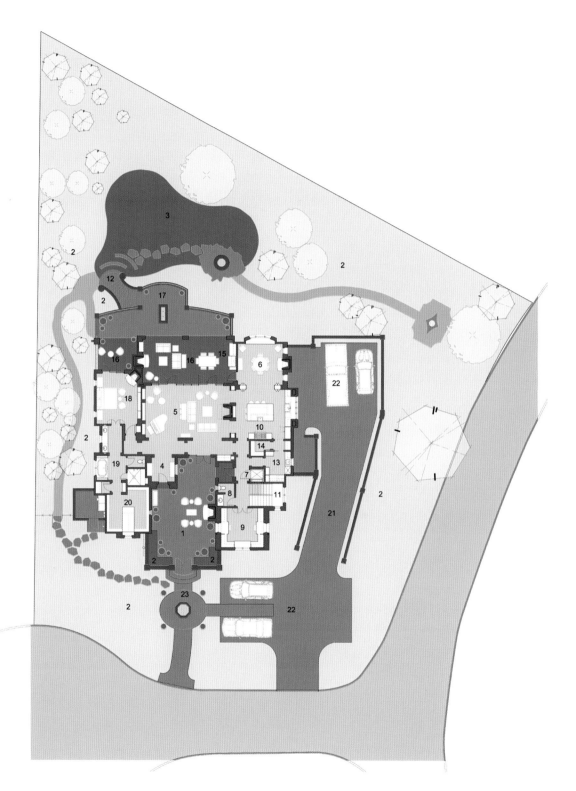

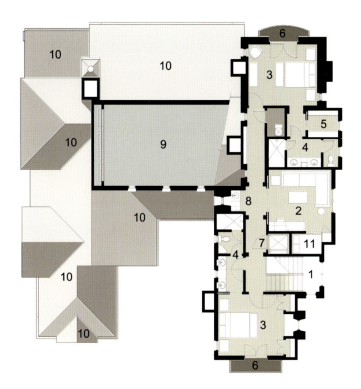

SECOND FLOOR

1. Main stairs
2. Lounge
3. Secondary bedroom
4. Bathroom
5. Closet
6. Balcony
7. Elevator
8. Morning bar
9. Open to below
10. Roof below
11. Bunk alcove

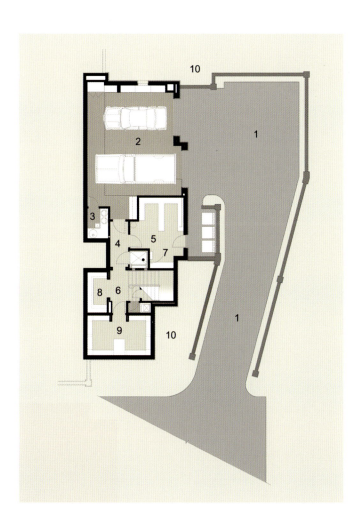

LOWER LEVEL

1. Auto court
2. Garage
3. Water system room
4. Garage vestibule
5. Garage storage
6. Stair vestibule
7. Elevator
8. Storage
9. Wine cellar
10. Garden

GAGE RESIDENCE

Spanish Colonial at Silverleaf

Matt and Jennifer Gage's five-bedroom residence sits on a corner lot in the Arcadia neighborhood of Silverleaf, adjacent to the McDowell Sonoran Preserve with its world-class views. The Gages, who have Midwestern roots, chose a lot overlooking a quiet landscaped island that reminded them of middle-America neighborhoods. However, to bring the parcel into compliance with new FEMA flood-prevention guidelines, we had to truck in 8 feet of fill and set the two-story home on top.

Neighboring homes had been built years prior to this new requirement, putting this house higher out of the ground than its neighbors. We brought in landscape designer Jeff Berghoff to terrace the gardens and trees up to the pad to ground it on the site and connect it with the neighborhood. Another challenging aspect of the corner property was its rhombus shape. To make this work, we struck a central axis from the street through the home's entry and out to a private rear courtyard.

The breakfast room towers to a clamshell multifaceted ceiling that fills the space with natural light. The drum chandelier repeats the circular shape of the table.
Photo courtesy of Rick Brazil

Although the house sits nearly 8 feet above street grade, the terraced gardens and fountains soften the composition.
Photo courtesy of Rick Brazil

The horseshoe-shaped house wraps around this courtyard, with the owner's suite on the one side and the great room, kitchen, and theater on the other side. A daughter's ensuite bedroom lies at the far end of the main floor. Upstairs, the office stacks above the owner's suite for privacy; the other three bedrooms stack over the far end of the house above the laundry and secondary bedroom suite, creating two distinct bedroom wings. As a result of this layout, the home wraps around a lovely courtyard, which allows it to receive abundant light from front to back.

Jeff's landscape design ties the house and gardens together with architectural staircases, fountains, and a front dining terrace. Among its diverse flora, the home includes hearty, drought-tolerant sissoo trees on the side facing the park, indigenous mesquites and agave, fruitless olive trees, and more than a hundred rose bushes.

Architectural styles are fairly prescriptive in this HOA community; among the limited offerings, the Gages chose Spanish colonial with its varying window shapes and arches. Inside, however, the aesthetic is crisper and lighter.

The first conceptual model of the Gage residence shows the retaining walls required to lift the house out of the floodplain.

The front façade of the Silverleaf home features a classic geometric Moorish stone fountain and carved stone entry surround; this establishes the primary axis from the front to the back courtyard.
Photo courtesy of Rick Brazil

The groin-vaulted dining room leads out to the front dining terrace through French doors. *Photo courtesy of Rick Brazil*

We collaborated with my wife, Isabel Dellinger-Candelaria, an interior designer and owner of Earth and Images, to create a variety of ceilings, such as the soaring groin vault in the dining room and a compound groin vault in the octagonal breakfast room. Jennifer and Isabel worked together to source lighting and personalize the rooms with framed family photographs. The children's bedrooms were designed around a piece of artwork each child chose for their room.

Select finishes add pops of glam, such as a zinc countertop on the bar, honed marble kitchen countertops, a drum chandelier in the dining room, and, a pewter soaking tub in the primary suite. In the media room, where Jennifer indulges her cinematic passion, Isabel framed ten images of Hollywood stars including Marilyn Monroe, Clint Eastwood, Joan Crawford, and Sophia Loren.

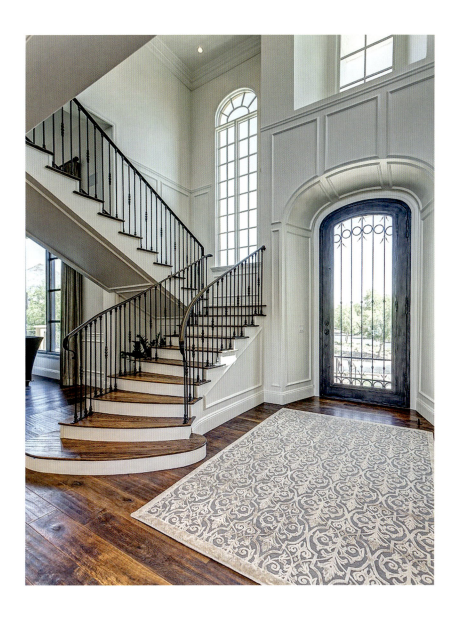

The stairway incorporates molding details that Isabel and Mark sketched on a construction photo for the carpenters. Because the home is elevated above the street, the large arched window at the landing provides extensive views across the front yard and into the community. The floor is European oak. *Photo courtesy of Rick Brazil*

Featuring a coffered ceiling and a teal finish, the upstairs office contains photos of vintage automobiles. *Photo courtesy of Rick Brazil*

The great room incorporates a zinc bar inspired by a local restaurant. The glam entertaining area opens to the inner courtyard. *Photo courtesy of Rick Brazil*

The bright, all-white kitchen opens to the great room and breakfast room, which connects to the inner courtyard. The matching ball pendants above the island are banded in pewter. *Photo courtesy of Rick Brazil*

A movie lover, Jennifer spends many hours in the theater room, complete with a vintage popcorn machine. Mounted on the back wall are photos of Hollywood legends such as Clint Eastwood, Goldie Hawn, Marilyn Monroe, Robert Redford, Audrey Hepburn, and Sophia Loren. *Photo courtesy of Rick Brazil*

The boat ride home from a day in Capri during the 2015 Candelaria Design Tour Italy included (*back row*): Isabel's first clients, Phil Giltner (*on the left*) and wife Renee (*on the right*), with Jennifer Gage (*in the middle*). In the front are Matt Gage and Isabel Dellinger-Candelaria.

TIRAMISU

Tiramisu is always a crowd favorite after a good meal. It's light and delicious and goes great with a cup of espresso or a glass of Vin Santo. We served this as a grand finale in a dinner with the Gages, on a hand-painted plate from Umbria.

SERVES 8–10

INGREDIENTS

Zabaglione

2 tablespoons heavy cream

¼ cup semisweet chocolate chips

4 large egg yolks

⅓ cup sugar

⅓ cup Marsala wine or Vin Santo

pinch of salt

Tiramisu

8 ounces mascarpone cheese

¾ cup heavy cream

⅔ cup sugar, divided

2 cups coffee or espresso

32 Savoiardi ladyfinger cookies

unsweetened cocoa powder and powdered sugar to sprinkle on top

PREPARATION

Zabaglione

1. Warm the heavy cream in a sauce pan over medium heat. Remove from the heat, add the chocolate chips, and stir until smooth. Keep warm.

2. In a metal bowl add the sugar, egg yolks, pinch of salt, and Marsala wine, and whisk.

3. Put about 2 inches of water in a large pot and heat until steaming, but not boiling. Place the metal bowl over the pot and keep whisking the mixture until it is thick like a custard and a thermometer reads 160°F. Don't let the eggs scramble! Whisk away.

4. When the temperature reaches 160°F, take the metal bowl off the heat and whisk a bit more so the custard is nice and thick like a soupy pudding.

5. Fold in the chocolate chip mixture and chill the metal bowl in the fridge. This makes a great dessert on its own with fruit or cookies.

Tiramisu

1. Using an electric mixer, whip the heavy cream and ⅓ cup of the sugar into stiff peaks. Then stir in the mascarpone and the chilled zabaglione mixture until smooth.

2. Line a 9½" × 5" × 2¼" bread pan with plastic wrap.

3. Dissolve remaining ⅓ cup sugar in the coffee. Dip one ladyfinger cookie at a time into the coffee very quickly so they do not get soggy, and line the bottom of the pan with the sugar side of the cookie down.

4. Spread half the zabaglione mixture over the top with a spatula. Then add another layer of dipped cookies. Top with the final half of the zabaglione mixture and then a final third layer of dipped cookies.

5. Wrap the whole thing with plastic wrap and let sit in the fridge for about 6 hours to set. When ready to serve, unwrap the top, flip the pan over on a decorative plate, and remove the plastic wrap from the bottom (now the top). Sift some unsweetened cocoa and powdered sugar over the top, slice and serve!

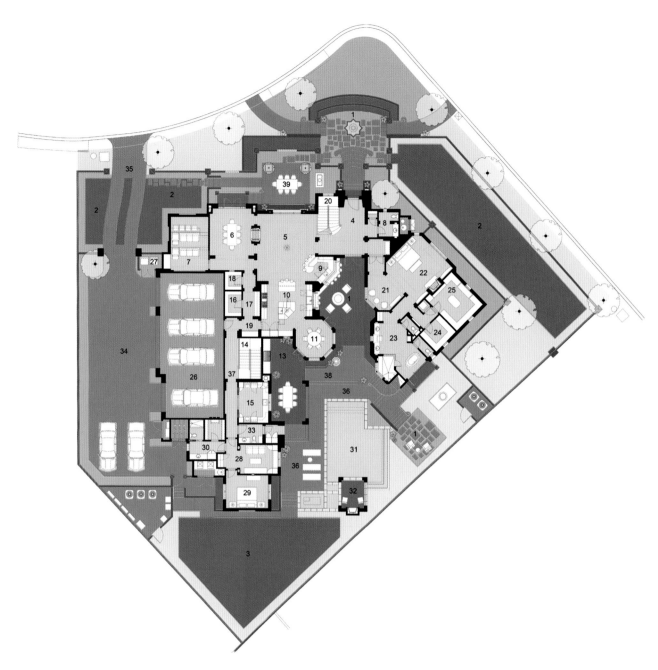

FIRST FLOOR

1 Courtyard	14 Back stairs	27 Trash enclosure
2 Garden	15 Laundry	28 Guest living
3 Lawn	16 Pantry	29 Guest bedroom
4 Foyer	17 Butler's pantry	30 Guest bathroom
5 Living room	18 Wine room	31 Pool
6 Dining room	19 Keydrop	32 Ramada
7 Theater room	20 Main stairs	33 Pool bath
8 Powder room	21 Primary bedroom sitting	34 Motor court
9 Bar	22 Primary bedroom	35 Driveway
10 Kitchen	23 Primary bathroom	36 Deck
11 Breakfast nook	24 Primary closet	37 Hallway
12 Lounge	25 Primary closet	38 Grand terrace
13 BBQ	26 Garage	39 Dining terrace

SECOND FLOOR

1. Main stairs
2. Hallway
3. Office
4. Back stairs
5. Secondary bedroom
6. Bathroom
7. Closet
8. Balcony
9. Terrace
10. Lounge area
11. Open to below
12. Roof below
13. Outdoor stairs

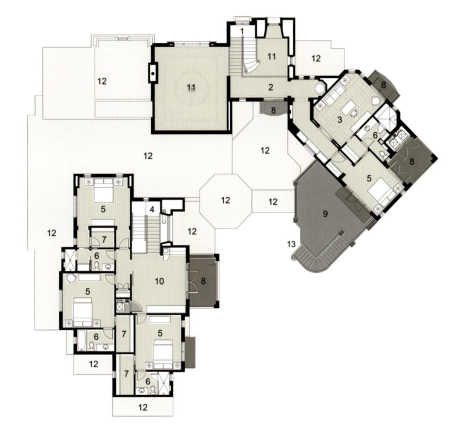

A conceptual rendering depicts the raised terrace by Bergdoff Design.

LANGE RESIDENCE

Compass Point to Camelback

When we met them in 2013, David and Linda Lange had already lived in two homes we had designed for other people. The first was a spec house in the Silverleaf community commissioned by luxury builder John Schultz. In their second move, they found one of our Santa Barbara–style houses for sale in Paradise Valley, closer to the urban amenities of central Scottsdale. Now, however, they called on us to create their own version of a dream home.

The 1-acre property they found was situated between Camelback Mountain to the south, where the couple hiked as children, and Mummy Mountain on the north. The corner lot contained a tired 1960s-vintage ranch-style home whose backyard faced Camelback Mountain. The home and property were reasonably priced, mainly because overgrown trees and oleander hedges obscured the mountain view.

Having lived in traditional homes, they were ready for something modern but weren't sure how far to take it. We drew two elevation studies, one with flat rooflines, horizontal elements, and lots of glass, and the other a contemporary Arizona ranch style that incorporated some traditional elements. They chose the latter, which became the vision that guided the design.

The four-bedroom, four-and-a-half-bathroom, one-level home mixes steel, locally quarried DC Cobblestone, wood, glass, and thick-textured Trenwyth concrete block. The latter material became the home's organizing structural element, directing sight lines toward Camelback Mountain, including its Praying Monk formation. The two primary interior fireplace walls, one in the great room and one in the owner's suite, extend from inside to outside, reinforcing this connection. Patios and courtyards abundantly showcase these views.

On the kitchen side of the house is the owners' suite, a comfortable wing for the empty-nesters. Their closet connects to a four-car garage and a large auto court for convenient access to everyday and collector cars. A butt-glazed corner window frames views of Camelback Mountain, and the steel and textured-concrete fireplace completes the tableau. An adjacent outdoor shower offers another invitation to step outside.

Previous page: The rear of the house opens to a cobalt-blue-tiled zero-edge infinity pool and a fire pit, maximizing views of Camelback Mountain, with Mummy Mountain to the north as a backdrop. *Photo copyright by Mark Boisclair*

The front façade celebrates the connection of interior to exterior. *Photo copyright by Mark Boisclair*

In the great room, steel truss beams ascend and intersect at the ceiling pitch, which is aligned with landmark Camelback Mountain, like a compass point. *Photo copyright by Mark Boisclair*

A corner window in the owners' suite frames views of Camelback Mountain. The flooring is reclaimed oak, and the walls are Trendwyth masonry. *Photo copyright by Mark Boisclair*

Both the kitchen and adjoining great room have window walls that open to the outdoor kitchen, barbecue, fire pit, zero-edge pool, and Camelback Mountain. In the great room, steel truss beams ascend and intersect at the ceiling pitch, which is precisely aligned with the mountain peak. All of our homes are designed along axis lines, and here the compass point is Camelback.

Other rooms include an office at the front of the house with vaulted wood ceilings, the dining room with a cobblestone and concrete fireplace and views of Mummy Mountain, and an exercise room and guest bedroom. The hallways, too, received special attention with steel beams and indirect lighting details.

The back elevation features multislide doors and windows that connect the great room and kitchen to the outdoors. *Photo copyright by Mark Boisclair*

Exposed steel beams and stained alder ceilings offer warmth and texture. Lighting designer Walter Spitz provided indirect light in the hallway, with spot accents on the artwork. *Photo copyright by Mark Boisclair*

The kitchen's alder wood trusses and wood ceiling complement the reclaimed oak wood floors. Charcoal-hued cabinetry, a custom walnut-slab table, matching drum lights above the island, and earth-tone, linen-upholstered chairs soften the edges. *Photo copyright by Mark Boisclair*

Interior designer Claire Ownby and lighting designer Walter Spitz collaborated to blend the couple's style preferences. Dave feels most comfortable with a modern aesthetic, while Linda prefers an organic and tactile interior. As a result, the structure and spatial feel of the home is clean-lined and crisp, but inside the materials and artwork add color and textural contrasts. There's nothing trendy in this home, just comfortable, functional spaces and materials that will retain their elegance for many years.

The dining room features a DC Cobblestone fireplace and a floor-to-ceiling view of Mummy Mountain. The great room's trapezium windows are repeated here to bring in consistent southern light. Linen draperies soften the look of a walnut and steel custom table. *Photo copyright by Mark Boisclair*

The owners enjoy an unobstructed view of Camelback Mountain across the zero-edge pool from the covered patio, an extension of the great room. *Photo copyright by Mark Boisclair*

The hallway connects the home's spaces and features crossovers and indirect lighting to create rhythm and cadence. The material palette features steel, concrete block, wood, DC Rubble stone, and glass. *Photo copyright by Mark Boisclair*

Client Dave Lange, builder John Schultz, and Mark join the Scottsdale Charros, a civic group promoting education, on the Arizona range during the annual Charro Ride fundraising event.

FETTUCINE VONGOLE WITH CHORIZO

This is a super-fast recipe and a real crowd pleaser. The chorizo gives this dish a kick!

SERVES 6

INGREDIENTS

1 pound fettucine

½ cup olive oil

2 tablespoons butter

1 shallot, minced

⅓ cup chopped Spanish chorizo or Italian salami

6 cloves garlic, minced

⅓ cup dry white wine

¼ cup fresh squeezed lemon juice

18-24 little neck clams

kosher salt and finely ground fresh pepper

1 tablespoon chopped fresh Italian parsley

1 teaspoon or a dash of red chili flakes

lemon wedge for garnish

PREPARATION

1. Bring a large pot of salted water to a boil and cook the pasta, per the package instructions, until al dente.

2. At the same time, in a high-sided saucepan set over medium-high heat, warm the olive oil and butter. Add the shallots and garlic and the chorizo and let this all literally melt and soften together for about 2 minutes.

3. Add the white wine and allow it to reduce about 1 minute. As the wine reduces, add the lemon juice and the clams and their juice. Stir everything together. Place a lid on the saucepan to steam the clams.

4. Check on the clams often, removing them as they open and placing them in a metal bowl with a foil lid to keep them warm. Keep steaming the clams until the last one opens.

5. Add the cooked linguini to the broth left in the saucepan. Add the clams back in and toss the mixture together, coating the linguine with the broth and distributing the clams.

6. Serve, garnished with chopped parsley, red chile flakes, and a lemon wedge. Make sure to add extra broth and a drizzle of olive oil to the pasta. Grate some fresh Parmesan cheese on top and add a dash of salt and pepper. Serve immediately.

The Langes selected the conceptual elevation of a modern Arizona ranch style, which combines the wife's preference for a natural, organic feeling and the husband's preference for a crisper lines. Camelback Mountain is shown behind it.

Lange Residence • Floor Plan

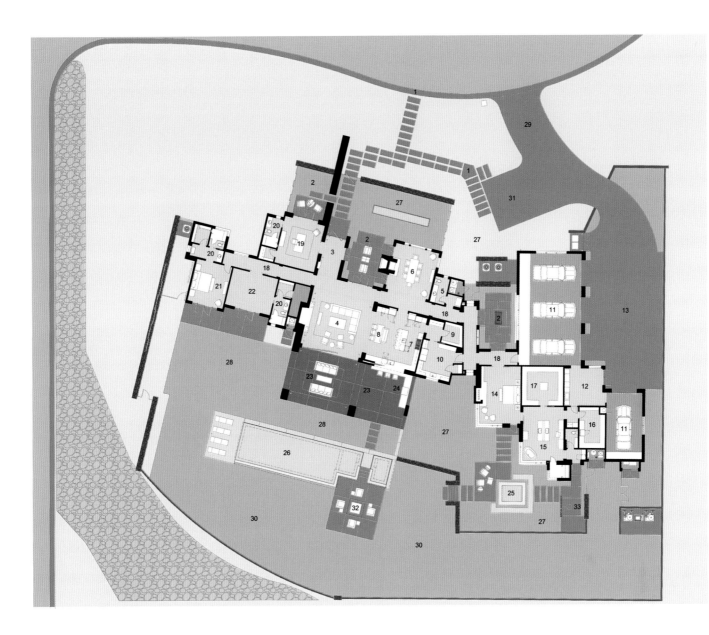

1	Access pathway	12	Workshop	23	Covered patio
2	Courtyard	13	Motor court	24	BBQ
3	Foyer	14	Primary bedroom	25	Spa
4	Living room	15	Primary bathroom	26	Pool
5	Powder room	16	Primary closet	27	Garden
6	Dining room	17	Primary closet	28	Lawn
7	Kitchen	18	Hallway	29	Driveway
8	Nook	19	Office	30	Landscaped area
9	Pantry	20	Bathroom	31	Guest parking
10	Laundry	21	Guest bedroom	32	Fire pit
11	Garage	22	Exercise	33	Outdoor shower

SCHULTZ RESIDENCES

Two of a Kind in Paradise Valley

John Schultz has a long history with our firm, having built many Candelaria homes and joined one of our Italy tours. So when he and his wife found a corner lot on which to build in Paradise Valley, close to their existing home, our partnership was a natural fit. We formed a team with Mesa interior designer Caroline DeCesare, and Scottsdale landscape designer Jeff Berghoff.

The Schultzes requested a traditional-style home built with natural materials such as stone, reclaimed wood, and a slate roof.

The front façade of the first of two Schultz homes in Paradise Valley consists of Kansas Rubble stone and a slate roof. These materials are enhanced by a bluestone walkway flanked by Mediterranean-inspired plantings. *Photo courtesy of Pearl Blossom Photography*

The front façade and lawn of the first Schultz residence reveals the artistry and architecture of Jeff Berghoff's landscape design. *Photo courtesy of Pearl Blossom Photography*

A central stone-clad volume marks the entrance to the "Z" shaped house. Inside, the foyer marks the cross-axis of an internal gallery and forms a transparent link between the front and back of the house. Essentially, you can walk into the house and right back out to the backyard. On one side of the foyer is the owner's suite and office; on the other is a dining room, kitchen, and great room, which opens to a large covered veranda. A breakfast pavilion acts as a focal point at the end of the main gallery and is surrounded by the gardens.

Passionate about cozy, country-inspired elements, the clients incorporated antique panels into the entry ceiling and John's office door, and laid reclaimed wood floors throughout and terra-cotta tile in the breakfast nook. A limestone fireplace surround anchors the great room, and a found antique door with an operable awning opens into their bedroom, announcing the arrival to this private space.

Reclaimed and found objects from the Schultzes' travels were incorporated into the home by interior designer Caroline DeCesare. An antique rolling door closes off the owners' suite, and an antique barn door opens to the shared office with reclaimed wood beams and hand-scraped European white oak floors. *Photo courtesy of Pearl Blossom Photography*

The kitchen's traditional white cabinetry is warmed by an oversized walnut-topped island, reclaimed-beam ceiling, and wood floors. The island's light fixtures were custom made to duplicate antiques the owners found on their travels. The breakfast room pavilion is visible through the archway. Its ceiling cove hides electronic shades and uplighting, and the flooring is antique terra-cotta tile. *Photo courtesy of Pearl Blossom Photography*

Large multislide doors open from the great room to a large outdoor patio and garden. The indoor/outdoor bar was one of our first residential examples; a few years earlier, we had designed a bar similar to this for the LEED Gold renovation of the 1930's El Chorro Restaurant and Bar in Paradise Valley.

In the kitchen, we designed cottage white–painted cabinets and an oversized island to contrast with the reclaimed wood-beam ceiling; these details and others made this the Houzz Kitchen of the Year. It connects to a light-suffused pavilion breakfast room with a crowning cupola and chandelier; just outside is the courtyard and the garden adjacent to the cul-de-sac.

The great room opens to the kitchen, and bifold stacking doors access the outdoor patio and bar. A two-hundred-year-old, oversized antique stone fireplace found in France anchors the space. *Photo courtesy of Pearl Blossom Photography*

The zinc-topped bar opens to the great room on the right and the covered patio on the left, where the windows pocket away to create a bar-length opening.
Photo courtesy of Werner Segarra

The east garden off the breakfast pavilion beckons for morning coffee or al fresco dinners under the iron arbor. *Photo courtesy of Werner Segarra*

The bar's black granite countertops have a leather finish, and the patio flooring is antique terra-cotta tile. *Photo courtesy of Pearl Blossom Photography*

In January 2018, the couple sold the property and asked Mark for help with another corner parcel they had purchased a mile or so away, also in Paradise Valley. Here they razed the older home and simplified the grounds and upkeep while recycling most of the original design on the differently oriented new lot.

It is interesting to experience the flip of the house and how it changes your perception of space, given my memories of the original home, but their new home is fantastic too. "This home duplicated 70 percent, plus or minus, of the original design, so about 30 percent was customized to meet the revised lot configuration and John and Denise's preferences," says Jeffrey G. Kramer, who led the design for this second home.

"We flipped the house, as the other lot was also on a corner but the reverse exposure," John explains. "The general feel of the home is very similar, with decorative touches being changed, such as the kitchen ceiling, which is brick in this house. Details were fine-tuned on all items;

The rear patio is oriented to receive afternoon shade. *Photo courtesy of Pearl Blossom Photography*

Next page: For the second home they built in Paradise Valley, the Schultzes requested exterior materials similar to those of the first house. Here they added drought-tolerant landscaping. *Photo courtesy of Pearl Blossom Photography*

The kitchen in the second house features a herringbone brick ceiling set above the reclaimed beams. *Photo courtesy of Pearl Blossom Photography*

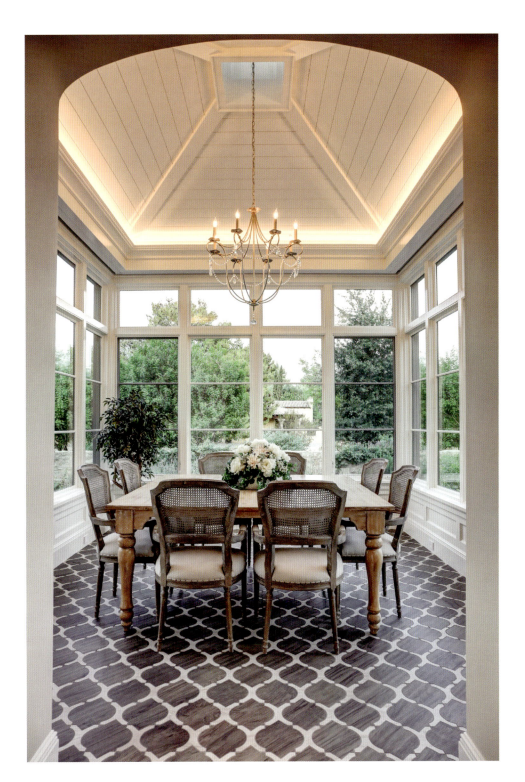

The cupola-topped breakfast room pavilion of the second Schultz home connects with the garden for sunlit breakfasts or intimate dinners. The same ceiling cove detail hides electronic shades and uplighting that highlights the ceiling. The flooring in this home is porcelain tile that mimics a wood pattern from Craftsman Court Ceramics in Scottsdale.
Photo courtesy of Pearl Blossom Photography

after living in the other house, we were able to really dial things in. Finally, the landscape is completely different in design and feel from the earlier home, incorporating a more drought-resistant plant palette." By flipping the home on the second home the breakfast room switched from the west side of the house to the east side of the house with its softer morning light. The owner's suite then correspondingly switched to the west side of the house using the owner's closet as the west sun blocker. Both homes had the front of the house facing south and the back to the north so that didn't change.

The back terrace of the home incorporates exterior materials such as reclaimed wood beams and posts from Canada, DC Rubble stone walls, and a slate roof; these are complemented by hedges, vines, potted plants, and a water feature. *Photo courtesy of Pearl Blossom Photography*

Owner/builder and architect celebrate the finished home. *Photo courtesy of Pearl Blossom Photography*

HERB-CRUSTED SMOKED PRIME RIB AND STEAMED LOBSTERS

My wife, interior designer Isabel Dellinger-Candelaria, and I love getting together with John and Denise. One of our favorite meals is prime rib, and when you can add a couple of lobsters and vegetables, it's that much better.

8–10 SERVINGS

INGREDIENTS

Herb-Crusted Prime Rib

1 6–8-pound bone-in or boneless prime rib roast

Marinade

6 cloves garlic, minced

1–2 tablespoons fresh rosemary

1–2 tablespoons fresh thyme

½ cup fresh Italian parsley, coarsely chopped

2 medium shallots

2 tablespoons red wine vinegar

½ cup olive oil

½ cup red wine

2 tablespoons salt for the marinade

Herb Crust and Rub

1 large shallot, coarsely chopped

6 garlic cloves, quartered

3 tablespoons minced fresh rosemary

2 tablespoons minced fresh oregano

2 tablespoons minced fresh thyme

2 tablespoons minced fresh sage

2 tablespoons olive oil

2 teaspoons salt for the prime rib crust

3 teaspoons ground black pepper

your favorite spice rub

4–6 tablespoons herbed butter to top grilled roast

Boiled Lobster and Veggies

2 whole lobsters and/or crab legs and claws

4 or 5 bay leaves

2–4 artichokes trimmed/halved and chokes cleaned out

6–8 small corn on the cobs, split in half

12 baby red potatoes

2–3 peeled onions, halved or quartered

6 quartered lemons

6 whole unpeeled garlic cloves

satchel of Old Bay seasoning

1–2 cups dry white wine

2–3 smoked andouille sausages (grill first to get grill marks and then slice into 1-inch pieces)

Horseradish Cream Sauce for the Prime Rib

½ cup heavy cream

½ cup sour cream

4 tablespoons freshly grated horseradish

2 tablespoons chives

6 tablespoons fresh squeezed lemon juice

salt and pepper to taste

PREPARATION

Prime Rib

1. Prepare the marinade. In a food processor, combine the rosemary, thyme, garlic, shallots, parsley, red wine vinegar, olive oil, red wine, salt, and pepper and pulse until well combined. Then put the prime rib in a large freezer bag or large pan and pour the marinade over the prime rib, rubbing it into every nook and cranny. Cover and refrigerate 6 to 24 hours.

2. Remove the meat from the refrigerator. Coat it with salt and let it sit for an hour to come to room temperature. After an hour, rinse the salt away and generously coat the prime rib with your favorite seasoning rub.

3. In a food processor, combine the first six ingredients from the herb crust list and pulse until finely chopped. Add the olive oil, salt, and pepper and process until well blended. Rub this herb and oil paste all over the prime rib and let it sit for another 20–30 minutes.

4. I like to put my prime rib in a roasting pan, so I collect the drippings and put everything in my Traeger smoker set to 275°F. Roast until the meat thermometer reads 125°F when inserted into the middle of the roast. Generally, it takes 15–20 minutes per pound, or about 2½ hours for an 8-pound roast, but be patient. When the temperature is reached, take the roast off the grill and cover with herbed butter, and then tent with foil and let rest for at least 15 minutes.

Note: As an alternative to the horseradish cream sauce, you can combine a half cup of the drippings with 1½ cups of beef broth and 1 cup of red wine and cook until reduced to about a cup of liquid. Add 1 teaspoon of butter and a pinch of salt.

Horseradish Cream Sauce

In an electric mixer, beat the heavy cream until stiff. With the mixer running, add the sour cream, horseradish, chives, lemon juice, and salt and pepper.

Steamed Lobsters

1. Put a big stock pot on a propane stand and fill it with 3 gallons of water. Bring this to a boil and add a generous amount of sea salt, bay leaves, and the satchel of Old Bay seasoning.

2. Add 6 quartered lemons and return the water to a boil. Once boiling again, add the 4 trimmed and halved artichokes with the chokes removed.

3. Cover the pot and let this boil for 10–15 minutes, and then add a dozen baby red potatoes, 6–8 ears of corn split in half, and 2–3 onions peeled and quartered. Reduce to simmer for 5 minutes, then add 6 whole unpeeled heads of garlic and 1–2 cups of your favorite dry white wine. Simmer covered until the veggies are tender.

4. About 40 minutes after the artichokes go in the water, remove the veggies, place them on a serving platter, and cover with foil to keep warm.

5. Grill two or three andouille sausages, slice them into nice-sized discs, and toss them in the boil. Let the sausage boil for about three minutes. Then add the live lobsters and any other shellfish you want to add, and boil for about 15 minutes.

6. Remove the lobsters, place in a colander, and rinse under cool running water to stop the cooking. Remove the sausage and add to the veggie platter, and top the platter with the lobsters. Serve side by side with the prime rib, and enjoy!

1	Courtyard	17	Storage
2	Garden	18	Back kitchen
3	Lawn	19	Garage
4	Foyer	20	Studio
5	Great room	21	Hallway
6	Dining room	22	Primary bedroom
7	Trellis	23	Primary bathroom
8	Powder room	24	Primary closet
9	Bar	25	Primary closet
10	Kitchen	26	Secondary bedroom
11	Breakfast nook	27	Bathroom
12	Lounge	28	Service powder
13	Covered patio	29	Wine room
14	Laundry	30	Vestibule
15	Workshop	31	Pool
16	Pantry	32	Guesthouse

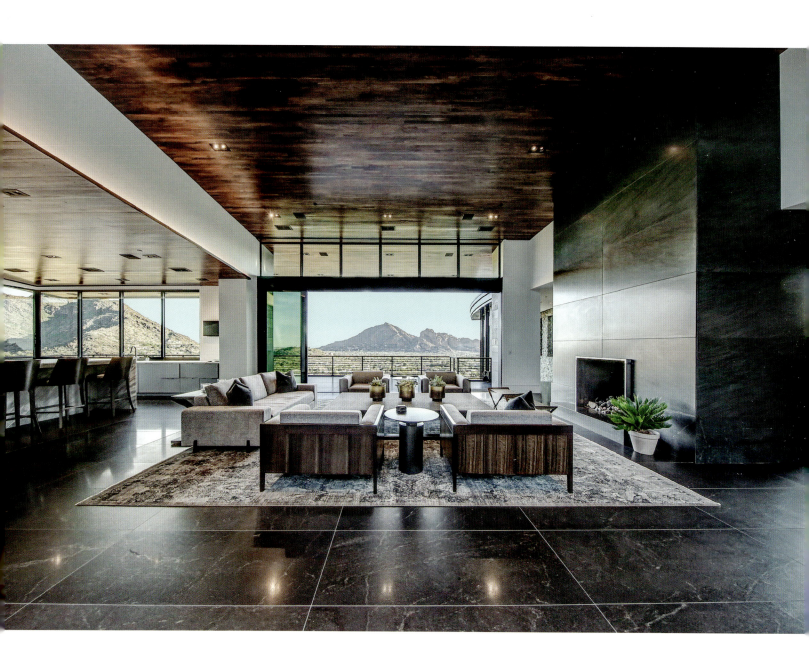

JOHNSON RESIDENCE

Hillside Contemporary

Much of the Phoenix area is a desert valley, so when even a slight elevation occurs, views are extensive. Hillside lots, in particular, offer this opportunity, but with it come challenges. This five-bedroom, modernist home in Paradise Valley for Steve and Donna Johnson was a prime example.

The project came to us through Scottsdale Realtors Mark and Chrissy Donnelly, whose clients wanted to sell the property adjacent to their home. The steep hillside lot contained an older home that failed to take advantage of the views, so potential buyers were struggling to see the possibilities. In addition, because of the restrictive community building codes, the agents worried that buyers would be intimidated by the time and paperwork necessary to comply.

Public spaces open dramatically to views of Camelback Mountain. Finishes and furnishings include stone and wood, a hand-knotted Indian wool rug sourced at David Adler, and a custom table with a Black Flannel granite top quarried in Zimbabwe, sourced through Cactus Stone & Tile, and fabricated by Stockett Tile and Granite. *Photo courtesy of Pearl Blossom Photography*

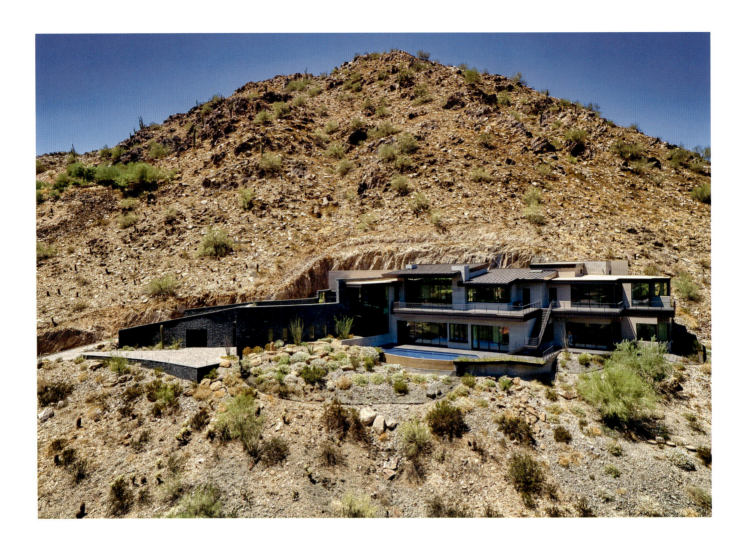

An aerial view shows the split-level underground garage and upper auto court to the left. The footprint is canted to optimize the Camelback Mountain views east and south. From the second level, the owner, an airline executive, loves to watch planes come and go from Sky Harbor International Airport. *Photo courtesy of Extreme Aerial Photography*

The lower driveway leads to the garage, which is directly below a public auto court. The curved black opal schist stone wall separates the garage and auto court from the house. In the distance to the north are the Carefree Mountains. *Photo courtesy of Pearl Blossom Photography*

Mark and Chrissy called to see if we would be willing to do some initial studies to paint those possibilities. So, we created plans and renderings of a luxury estate with multiple garages and a tennis court, showing buyers what could be accomplished in compliance with the demanding building code.

The Johnsons, who lived nearby in Paradise Valley, liked our ideas. Their existing home was hacienda-inspired Southwest style, but they wanted to shift toward a more glassy, modernist style to optimize the panoramic views of Camelback Mountain and flights arriving and leaving from Sky Harbor International Airport about 10 miles away.

Initially they were concerned that our firm is primarily known for traditional homes. However, we had just completed a modernist house

for the Langes, and the Johnsons admired a similarly styled home we'd designed for their friends nearby. That house, in fact, had nudged them toward a sleeker dwelling.

Working with builder Schultz Development, interior designer Anita Lang, landscape architects Greey | Pickett, and lighting designer Walter Spitz, we got to work on a design that would capture the 270-degree views on this amazing property. To do this, we needed to demolish the existing house and excavate the pad to extend the footprint as far as town code would allow.

John Schultz and his team cut nearly 30 feet of hillside, which required rock bolts to be inset and epoxied to stabilize the face of the mountain. Downhill retaining walls were also built for support on the hill. This was

The various decks and levels offer unique vistas from different rooms. *Photo courtesy of Pearl Blossom Photography*

The 12-foot-high backyard retaining wall is clad in black opal schist and serves as a base to the rock-bolted, native-cut slope. Designed by Greey | Pickett, the stone monolith water feature pours into a reflecting pool—all set on axis with the dining room and garden. "At night, the wall is washed with lighting and becomes a focal point," says landscape architect Russell Greey. *Photo courtesy of Pearl Blossom Photography*

The negative-edge pool, which seems to spill off the hillside, is set on axis with Camelback Mountain and acts as the organizing element for the house. *Photo courtesy of Pearl Blossom Photography*

The home opens to the hillside private garden in the back and views to Camelback Mountain on the other side, providing a full desert experience. Greey | Pickett worked with a desert plant palette including cactus, agave, succulents, and desert trees such as ironwood and palo verde, the state tree. *Photo courtesy of Pearl Blossom Photography*

accomplished with sensitivity to the terrain by stair-stepping the heights so they flow with the terrain and landscape. The house footprint had to be cut in on one side and filled on the other to create a balance between the cut and fill. Instead of the house being backed right up to the cut, however, we left patio space for light, air, water features, and landscape, which allowed the home to breathe from front to back and side to side.

Set against the Phoenix Mountain Preserve, the steep site presented other grading challenges to ensure that the ascent to the auto-court from the street was manageable. In addition, the construction team had to carefully plan the build sequence, because the nine-car underground garage and negative-edge pool had to be constructed before the house went up. To minimize the hillside disturbance, the team added a second driveway to the garage and placed the guest auto court at a higher

Stone floors, a walnut ceiling, and the black opal schist feature wall bring the outdoors in, while telescoping walls connect the hill on one side with valley views on the other. *Photo courtesy of Pearl Blossom Photography*

The kitchen has spectacular views of Paradise Valley, including Mummy Mountain to the east. The walnut plank ceiling continues the theme from the great room. *Photo courtesy of Werner Segarra*

Next spread: The dining room opens to the back garden with telescoping doors that vanish into the walls. The table is from Minotti, open-pore oak and a Moka finish, designed by Anita Lang. *Photo courtesy of Pearl Blossom Photography*

elevation over the top of the subterranean garage, thus stacking the uses to avoid disturbing more soil. Adjacent on this lower level is the son's bedroom and a recreation room that opens out to the pool, on axis with Camelback Mountain to the southeast.

From the parking court, visitors enter along a boulder-strewn pathway to the front door. The guest wing lies to the left along a curving hallway, while the family living spaces unspool to the north and east, flowing out to expansive terraces. The living room and kitchen continue into a glassy dining room on axis with a reflecting pool designed by Greey | Pickett within a cacti courtyard. Walter Spitz's dramatic lighting design illuminates the courtyard and hillside beyond. A third level at the back of the house contains Steve's office, which accesses a roof deck, and the owners' suite, with views as far north as Pinnacle Peak in Scottsdale. "For Steve, an airline executive, the view is king, and he particularly liked this site because he can see the planes coming and going," Donna says.

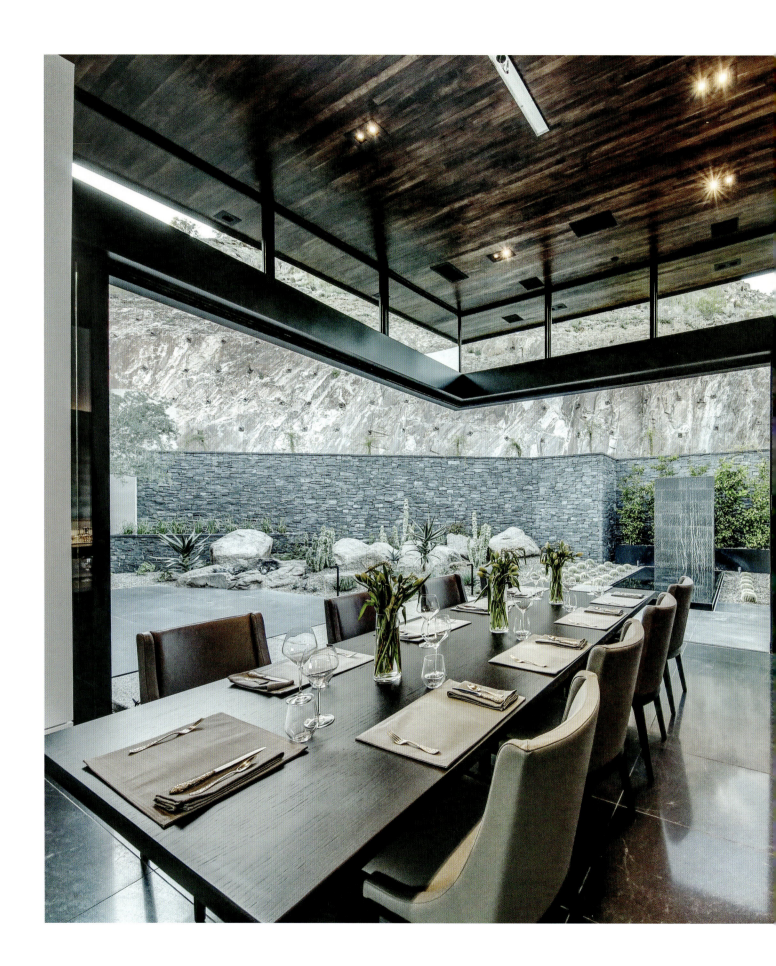

Steve and Donna were closely involved in their home's design and details, choosing natural materials inside and out, such as smooth and rough-faced stone and natural wood. A thick black opal schist wall separates the auto court from the home and acts as a contrasting façade from the driveway up the hill. The schist has a subtle sparkle that gives the home a distinctive glisten.

Interiors are comfort yet bespoke, with basalt floors, walnut wood ceilings for warmth against the gray elements Steve requested, and accessories such as designer rugs from David Adler in Scottsdale. The lower-level recreation room is anchored by a wine room with glass and metal racking set along the curved stone wall, and a steel-and-glass stair to the upper level—materials that retain their basic natures.

Previous page: In the owner's bath, a window wall dissolves the boundaries between indoors and out, and a vanity mirror reflects Camelback Mountain. *Photo courtesy of Pearl Blossom Photography*

Previous page: The glass, steel, and stone staircase anchors to the black opal schist wall connecting the two levels. Flooring is made of black hearth granite slabs. *Photo courtesy of Pearl Blossom Photography*

A metal and glass custom wine room defines one side of the room. The handwoven wool rug is from Afghanistan, sourced at David Adler in Scottsdale. *Photo courtesy of Werner Segarra*

Next spread: In front of the house, a negative-edge pool curves in the opposite direction of the landscape wall. Greey | Pickett revegetated the hillside with native plants. *Photo courtesy of Pearl Blossom Photography*

MARK'S SPANISH PAELLA

I love cooking for my clients, especially when I can cook in their home and the kitchen we created. We celebrated the completion of this home with my signature paella—the homeowners are from the Pacific Northwest and love seafood dishes. I learned to make this dish while visiting the north coast of Spain in the early 1990s and have made hundreds of paellas since then.

SERVES 8

INGREDIENTS

3 chicken legs

3 chicken thighs

1 teaspoon dried oregano

2 tablespoons smoked paprika

kosher salt and freshly ground pepper

¼ cup extra-virgin olive oil

1 handful of Spanish chorizo sausage

2 andouille sausages

4 garlic cloves, diced

1½ cups Pinot Grigio white wine

1 Spanish onion, diced

1 16-ounce can diced tomatoes

1½ cups arborio rice

1 teaspoon saffron threads

1 16-ounce box of chicken broth

1 16-ounce box of seafood broth

¼ cup Spanish sherry

6-8 jumbo shrimp with tails on, peeled and deveined

1 cod filet

1 lobster tail

6-8 clams, scrubbed

6-8 mussels, scrubbed and debearded

½ cup peas, thawed

flatleaf Italian parsley for garnish

lemon wedges for serving

PREPARATION

1. Wash and dry the chicken and cod, and season with the salt, pepper, paprika, and oregano. Let sit for 30 minutes.

2. Heat the oil in a paella pan and sauté the chicken until nicely browned on both sides. Remove and cover with foil to keep warm. Then do the same with the fish and sausages and set aside. Add more olive oil, if needed. When the sausages are done, slice them into ¼-inch-thick slices on the bias.

3. Add chopped onions and garlic to the pan, and deglaze with the white wine. Scrape up the bits and stir the onions and garlic until softened and translucent.

4. Add the tomatoes and bring to a gentle boil. Build a well in the middle and add the rice, frying it and slowly spreading it out to combine with the tomato and onion mixture.

5. Add the saffron strands and the broths, a cup at a time. Let the rice slowly absorb the broth, adding more as it gets absorbed. Let the rice cook for about 10 minutes to a perfect consistency—not too soupy and not too dry.

6. Break the fish filet into bite-size chunks and add to the paella along with the chicken, sausages, and shellfish. Tuck all of these ingredients into the paella and then set the lobster on the center. Sprinkle the Spanish sherry over the entire paella and place a lid on top. Let it simmer for 15–20 more minutes. Add more broth if too dry. If too soupy, uncover for a bit and let the liquid cook off.

7. During the last 5 minutes of cooking, scatter the peas over the paella for the bright green color. Remove from the heat and garnish with lemon and chopped parsley. Enjoy!

Photo courtesy of Pearl Blossom Photography

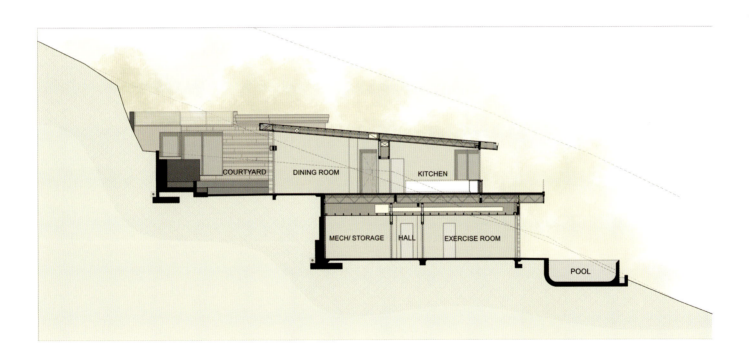

Mark's design-concept rendering optimizes views east and south to Camelback Mountain while maintaining an intimate relationship with the land.

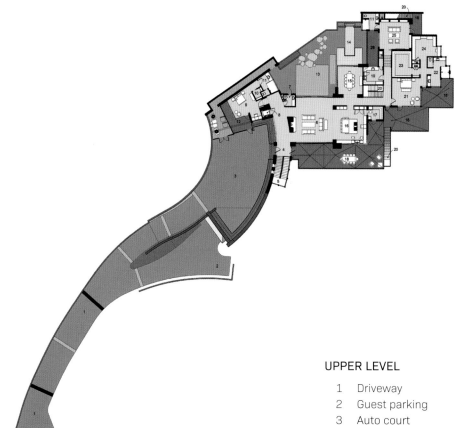

UPPER LEVEL

1. Driveway
2. Guest parking
3. Auto court
4. Entry
5. Main stairs
6. Great room
7. Powder room
8. Elevator
9. Guest room
10. Closet
11. Bathroom
12. Covered patio
13. Patio
14. Reflecting pool
15. Dining room
16. Kitchen
17. Pantry
18. Terrace
19. Laundry
20. Stairs
21. Primary bedroom
22. Primary bathroom
23. Primary closet
24. Primary closet
25. Office
26. Planter

Johnson Residence • Floor Plan

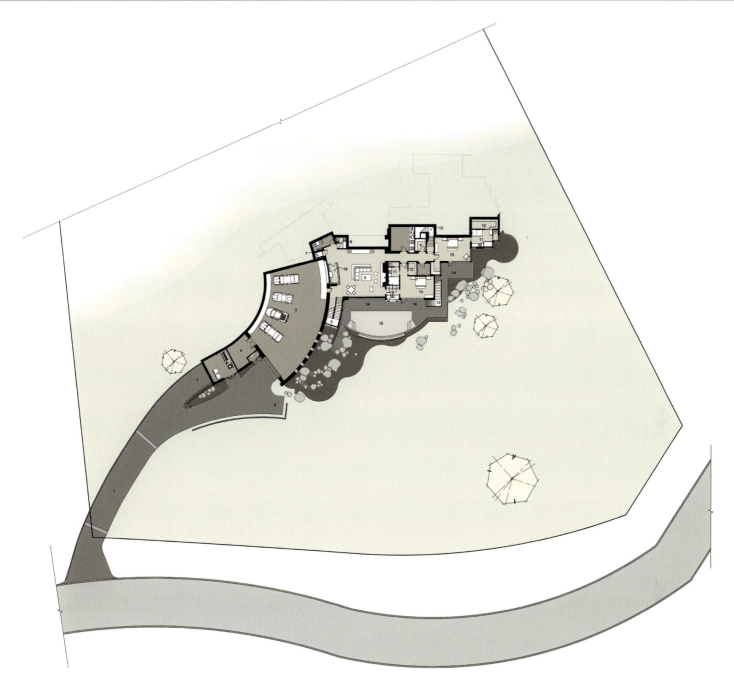

LOWER LEVEL

1. Driveway
2. Guest parking
3. Garage
4. Storage
5. Main stairs
6. Lounge area
7. Elevator
8. Powder room
9. Bar
10. Secondary bedroom
11. Bathroom
12. Closet
13. Stairs
14. Courtyard
15. Pool
16. Wine room

A pool, raised spa, and fire ring flow from the back of the house. In the background is Tonto National Forest. *Photo courtesy of Werner Segarra*

Phyllis Lerner fell in love with the antique doors at Porte del Passato in Umbria, Italy.

Master woodworkers Gabriele Belli (*left*) and his father, Enzo Belli (*right*) at their studio in Porte del Passato. Their team crafted the coffered ceiling for an office, the primary bedroom bookcase, the main entrance oak door, and interior doors.

LERNER RESIDENCE

European Villa at Desert Mountain

For twenty-one years, Phyllis and Gil Lerner lived in the Arrowhead Village of Desert Mountain, a golf course community in North Scottsdale. In 2005, they purchased a view lot in the Village of Saguaro Forest and became full-time Arizona residents after selling their home on Long Island, New York.

At an altitude of 3,000 feet, the property overlooks community golf courses, Scottsdale, and the valley beyond. The couple began cruising the area for inspiration for a new house. While searching Paradise Valley to the south, they noticed several Candelaria Design homes under construction that looked similar to what they were envisioning.

They wanted a European-style villa with courtyards, interior spaces that captured the views, and a backyard where they could entertain and enjoy the Arizona desert. In fact, we incorporate courtyards into virtually every home we design. Views are also a major driver of a home's layout. The views tell us where to place the various spaces and how to align them so that a visual cue is always present, conscious or subconscious, as one moves from space to space.

Phyllis also wanted every room to have a unique theme while remaining cohesive with the rest of the house. Armed with a large collection of images, we spent many hours sketching how we might incorporate their ideas into the design. The clients helped us fine-tune every detail of every room, from the diverse ceiling designs to the patterns in the floors.

Staking the site helped us refine the view corridors and the layout. Our team generated elevations and digitally modeled the home, which added to our clients' excitement.

Then came the Great Recession and a simultaneous shock wave. I will never forget the day I was meeting with Phyllis, and she was interrupted to take a call. Her face turned pale and she said, "We need to put this house on hold. Bernie Madoff just made off with our money!" We couldn't believe it, but just like that another project was back-burnered.

Mark's initial sketch of Gil's office suggests the many textures that make it a much-loved space.

Gil's office contains the wall panels and coffered wood ceiling made from three-hundred-year-old Umbrian poplar. Gabriele and his team visited the Lerners' home to measure for the pieces, then returned to Porte del Passado to fabricate them. After they were shipped to Scottsdale the following year, Gabriele returned with his craftsmen to assemble the office.
Photo courtesy of Werner Segarra

The formal dining room has paneled walls and a coved ceiling with a decorative glass laylight by Powers Brothers Stained Glass in Scottsdale. A clerestory provides additional light. Eclectically finished, the room contains many of the clients' memories, including the matching wood sconces above the hutch, which hung in Phyllis's mother's apartment in Queens, New York.
Photo courtesy of Werner Segarra

Phyllis invited Mark to join and cook for her birthday party at her home.

Four years later, Phyllis and Gil were ready to move ahead but decided to reduce the size from 12,000 to 8,300 square feet of living space, which ultimately improved the home. Groundbreaking occurred on April 1, 2014, and in September 2015, Phyllis joined us on a Candelaria Italy Tour. In Umbria, we introduced her to master craftsman Gabriele Belli, whose Porte del Passato studio curates reclaimed and reproduced antiquities, including millwork, doors, fireplaces, tiles, and other home components.

In particular, Phyllis was intrigued by the antique poplar-coffered ceiling Gabriele had created for his father's office. We began working with him and his team to create millwork for Gil's office and other areas in the home.

Gabriele visited the house to take measurements and then assembled the multiple pieces of Gil's study in his studio in Italy for us to inspect online. Shortly after, he shipped the custom oak main door and interior doors and the study components, which are constructed with 300-year-old poplar from Umbrian forests. Finally, Gabriele returned to the Lerners' home with two associates and worked with Manship Builders for a week to install the custom millwork.

Phyllis also wanted to incorporate a collection of photos from the couple's travels, such as a South African safari. "The interior is very traveled and eclectic," says Teresa Nelson, owner of Nelson Barnum Interiors, who helped place the photos, artwork, and furnishings.

Dual custom marble fireplaces anchor the living room, with its groin-vaulted ceiling. Matching fireplaces create two intimate seating areas, with a large-screen television between them. *Photo courtesy of Werner Segarra.*

One of the home's centerpiece spaces is the expansive great room, resplendent with natural light; we fitted it with a groin-vaulted ceiling and dual fireplaces for intimate entertaining. Adjacent is the kitchen with a brick and skylight ceiling and a copper-and-brass La Cornue range. Another striking room is the owners' bathroom suite, which features a sun-drenched octagonal spa pavilion with a latticed ceiling.

The Lerners remain close friends and have hosted us as overnight guests. It is a life-changing experience to go to sleep and wake up in one of our creations—especially with so many memories of making it happen. The project is a testament to endurance, commitment, and perseverance. For a dozen years, none of us gave up on the dream.

The skylit kitchen contains a La Cornue copper and brass cooktop, hand-rubbed alder cabinetry, a ceiling of white-washed brick set in a herringbone pattern, and handmade ceramic cooktop tiles. *Photo courtesy of Pearl Blossom Photography*

Kitchen sketch

The groin-vaulted brick, steel, and glass room is a great place to store and display the owner's vodka and wine collection. The barrel-oak racking is by Innovative Wine Cellar Design, Scottsdale. *Photo courtesy of Werner Segarra*

The octagon-shaped indoor spa off the owners' bathroom is resplendent with light and 180-degree views of the surrounding high desert. *Photo courtesy of Werner Segarra*

The sun-washed owners' suite has a vaulted ceiling with applied-trim walls. The canopy bed incorporates distressed wood and curtains trimmed in large checkered linen. The flooring is French white oak.
Photo courtesy of Werner Segarra

Connecting to all the major rooms of the home, the grand gallery is the cross axis for the main entry axis and consists of repetitive groin vaults. The flooring is Durango stone with 3-inch Thassos white marble medallions set between the larger tiles and as a border. The six sconces match the large living room chandelier.
Photo courtesy of Werner Segarra

The entry courtyard leads to the hand-carved old-oak front door from Umbria and its hand-carved stone portal surround by Contessa Stone Design, Scottsdale. The pavers are Durango stone, matching the interior flooring for a seamless transition from inside to out. *Photo courtesy of Pearl Blossom Photography*

BEEF TENDERLOIN WITH HONEY-GLAZED CARROTS

I prepared this dish in the Lerners' kitchen to celebrate Phyllis' birthday with thirty guests, with my daughter Tiffany and friends Rob English and Maxi Castillero as sous chefs. The honey-glazed carrots are a perfect vegetable pairing, and it never hurts to add some rosemary-and garlic–roasted hasselback potatoes.

SERVES 8

INGREDIENTS

Beef Tenderloin

1½ pounds beef tenderloin, trimmed, patted dry

salt and pepper to season generously

¼ cup or so of butter, softened

3 cloves minced garlic and 4 peeled whole cloves for roasting

2 tablespoons minced rosemary plus additional whole sprigs for roasting

1 tablespoon olive oil

1 cup red wine

½ cup beef broth

1 tablespoon balsamic vinegar

1 tablespoon cornstarch

1 tablespoon water

Honey-Glazed Carrots

1 pound baby carrots, stems trimmed to about ¼ inch

¼ cup olive oil

dusting of kosher salt

¼ cup brown sugar

¼ cup honey

4 tablespoons butter

4 sprigs thyme leaves, diced

flatleaf Italian parsley, diced

coarse salt sprinkle to finish

PREPARATION

Beef Tenderloin

1. Preheat oven to 400°F. Rub the beef tenderloin with the olive oil and season with salt and pepper.

2. In a small bowl, mix the minced garlic, rosemary, and butter and set aside.

3. Heat a large cast iron skillet over medium-high heat. Add 1 tablespoon of the butter and oil and melt to coat the pan. Place the beef tenderloin in the skillet and sear all sides until there is a nice brown crust.

4. Remove the tenderloin from the skillet and place in a baking dish. Brush with half of the garlic-rosemary butter and arrange the whole garlic cloves and rosemary around the tenderloin. Bake at 400°F for 20–25 minutes until the tenderloin reaches an internal temperature of 120°F–125°F.

5. Remove from the oven, place on a cutting board, and brush with the remaining garlic rosemary butter. Cover with foil and let rest for at least 10 minutes.

6. While the tenderloin rests, drain the drippings from the baking dish into the skillet. Add the red wine, stock, and vinegar. Bring to a slow simmer to reduce.

7. In a small bowl, whisk together equal parts cornstarch and water, and then slowly pour into the sauce and continue to whisk the sauce to thicken.

8. Slice the beef tenderloin into inch-thick pieces, plating two pieces per plate with one laid flat and the other tilted against the other. Drizzle on the wine sauce and add a sprinkle of coarse kosher salt or sea salt along with a sprinkle of diced parsley.

Honey-Glazed Carrots

1. Preheat oven to 400°F.

2. Wash and dry the carrots, and coat with olive oil in a baking dish. Sprinkle with salt. Place in the oven for 30–40 minutes or until they start to brown and slightly soften. Remove from the oven when done.

3. In a skillet over medium heat, combine the brown sugar, butter, honey, and thyme leaves. Add the carrots, coating them with the sauce. Sometimes I like to add some chopped pecans for a little crunch. Sauté the carrots for a few minutes until they are well coated but not mushy. Serve with the tenderloin and another sprinkle of salt and parsley.

A concept rendering of the rear façade shows its European villa details such as archways, high chimneys, a cupola, and stonework.

A computer model shows how the pool, spa, terrace, bocce court, and lower sitting area were incorporated into a challenging foothills lot.

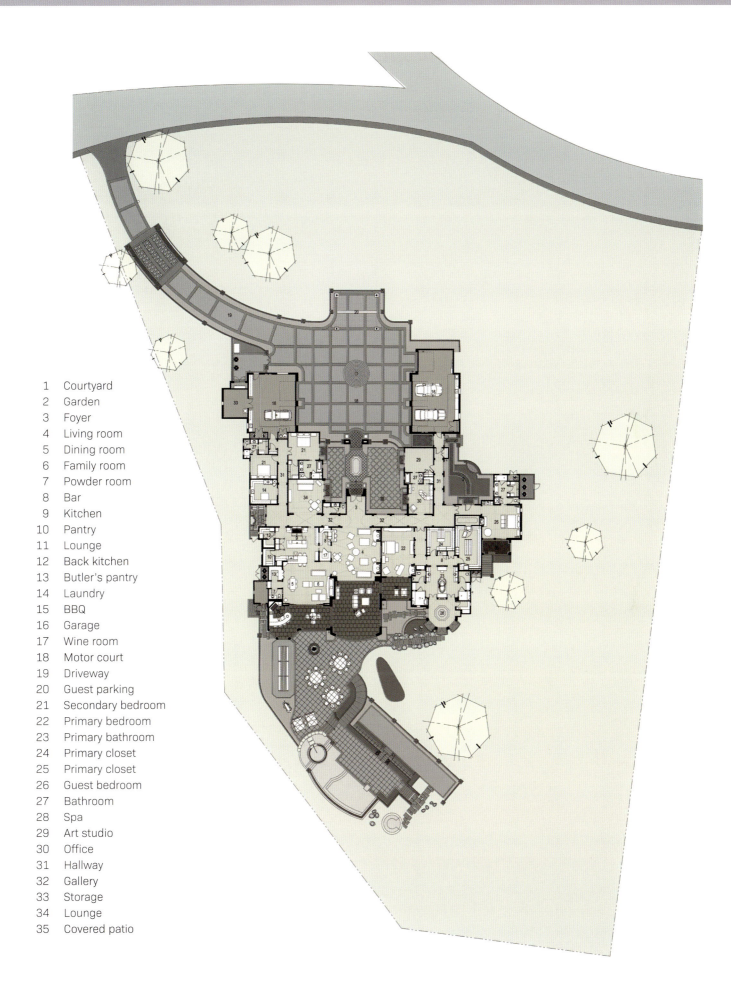

A sweeping road brings Larry Fitzgerald and his guests to the back of the property, which becomes the front of the home. This orientation allowed the back of the home to face Camelback Mountain.
Photo Courtesy of Werner Segarra

LARRY FITZGERALD RESIDENCE

French Manor Estate

The Paradise Valley home of Larry Fitzgerald, Arizona Cardinals star and one of football's all-time great wide receivers, was a high point of our two-decade-long practice. I clearly remember receiving the call from Larry's representative and designer, Sara Doto, of Longcross Partners. Isabel and I were in New York City for the annual New York Retail Market and were walking down Madison Avenue when I took the call. Her British accent only heightened the mystery of who her anonymous client might be.

Our team assembled a package showcasing our work and submitted it to Sara, who was in the process of interviewing architects coast to coast. A few weeks later I received a follow-up call from Sara, who disclosed the client's name. We arranged to take Sara, Larry, and one of his advisors on a tour of several CDA-designed homes in North Scottsdale and Paradise Valley.

Project architect (now partner) Meredith Thomson in front of the dining room pavilion wth steel sash doors. *Photo courtesy of Pearl Blossom Photography*

Renowned cabinet designer Christopher Peacock created the tailored oak cabinetry in the owner's bedroom closet; lighting designer Walter Spitz provided the LED and pendant lighting. *Photo courtesy of Pearl Blossom Photography*

Soon after, we were awarded the contract for his residence on a 3-acre parcel on the northeast side of Camelback Mountain. Sara was also interviewing landscape architects and builders to create a cohesive team. This is essential for any project, but especially for houses of this size; assembling the team early is critical to success. After reviewing the short list we provided of people who could successfully execute the highly detailed project, they asked the landscape firm Berghoff Designs and builder Shultz Development to join us.

Led by project architect Meredith Thomson, who is now a firm partner, our team fleshed out Larry's vision for the home, which has spectacular views of Camelback Mountain from most of the public and private spaces. First, though, we had to solve an orientation challenge: The street side of the property faced the primary view, Camelback Mountain, but Larry wanted to enjoy the view from a private back yard. The solution was to flip the floor plan and reorient the entry sequence

The great room joins with the kitchen, and both open to the outdoors. Initially the two rooms were more separated, but opening them up created a more engaging gathering space for entertaining. *Photo courtesy of Werner Segarra*

Next page: "We spent a lot of time making sure we had the house positioned just right, to capture the head of Camelback Mountain," says builder John Schultz. Along the view line from the outdoor patio is the backyard iron pool pavilion and a folly bath house. *Photo courtesy of Pearl Blossom Photography*

The office has a paneled wall, coffered alder ceiling, French white oak wood flooring set in a herringbone pattern, and a superb view. "We wanted the architecture, landscape, and furniture to work in harmony and not let one element overpower the others," Meredith says. *Photo courtesy of Pearl Blossom Photography*

The exterior stone cladding slips into the dining room, where a brick barrel ceiling and reclaimed oak beams gives the space an indoor-outdoor feel. "The primary goal was to create a sanctuary, a space for quiet and privacy and to reflect and recharge," says Sara Doto. *Photo courtesy of Werner Segarra*

with a long, hedge-enclosed driveway that sweeps around the side of the house to the entry near the back of the triangular-shaped lot. "The road guides you along the side of the property and turns you around at the back, which opens up the views in a dramatic way," says Meredith. "It really takes you out of Paradise Valley and makes you feel like you've traveled to a different country." In that way, the back of the house became the front and the street-facing side became the back, ensuring a perfectly framed "backyard" view of the iconic "camel head."

Having traveled extensively, Larry envisioned a French-inspired manor home, naming it "Longcross." He wanted something elegant and timeless, yet clean-lined and fresh. Specifically, he asked for a family-friendly sanctuary where he could relax with his children.

Reclaimed oak parquet wood floors and a hand-carved limestone fireplace anchor the living room. *Photo courtesy of Pearl Blossom Photography*

Expressing quiet softness, the owner's bedroom is a study in various tones of his favorite color, blue. These textiles complement the reclaimed limestone fireplace and artwork. *Photo courtesy of Pearl Blossom Photography*

A main gallery acts as the home's organizing spine. Bisected by the gallery, the foyer leads into the living room, with its spectacular views of Camelback Mountain. To the right, past the office, the northwest end of the gallery empties into a cross axis and courtyard that separates the owner's suite on the left, facing the mountain, from the children's bedrooms on the right, facing the front courtyard.

The southeast end of the main gallery leads to the family room and kitchen. At the midpoint between the kitchen and living room is a glass dining pavilion oriented toward the view. At the far south end of the home are two additional bedroom suites and the garages. The gallery creates sight lines down the halls, while adjacent courtyards and water features provide visual cues that place the occupants in the outdoors.

To design the kitchen, butler's pantry, and primary suite, the team, along with Larry, flew to Greenwich, Connecticut, to meet with renowned cabinet designer Christopher Peacock. Christopher calls the cabinetry and panel work in the owner's suite "masculine, grand, and gentlemanly," and the kitchen and butler's pantry "timeless and elegant like the owner."

The materials, all hand-selected, include limestone fireplace mantels carved from blocks sourced in France; stone flooring from a quarry in Bourgogne, France, that were custom cut and finished; French white oak parquet and chevron floors imported from Europe, handmade and finished in the old French style; solid oak reclaimed beams; a French wellhead repurposed as a fountain outside the dining room; reclaimed driveway pavers; and reclaimed French stone called third-face Dalle de Bourgogne for the main house exterior. The stone masons hand-chipped tens of thousands of pieces before placing them to achieve a one-off, random look. "It's rural French with a tailored refinement," Meredith says of the finished house.

The Christopher Peacock–designed kitchen combines reclaimed French oak beams and stone flooring. These materials add warmth, richness, and texture to the white cabinetry and stone countertops.
Photo courtesy of Werner Segarra

The great room spans the width of the house, connecting to the front and back gardens. French limestone fireplaces center the great room and great room porch, and reclaimed oak wood beams and stone flooring, also from France, add warmth and richness. *Photo courtesy of Pearl Blossom Photography*

The main gallery's cased openings with transoms form a cadence through the home. 'We were mindful of creating areas for artwork that would feel seamless and would be focal points, while ensuring a balance with the architecture, surfaces, and furniture," Sara says. *Photo courtesy of Werner Segarra*

Paved in Belgium cobblestones, the front auto court features a hand-carved limestone fountain. *Photo courtesy of Pearl Blossom Photography*

A hand-carved stone fountain and stone walls transport one to the French countryside. *Photo courtesy of Pearl Blossom Photography*

Next page: Dusk over Paradise Valley pairs well with outdoor lighting by Walter Spitz. *Photo courtesy of Werner Segarra*

BEEF POT ROAST WITH MUSHROOM RISOTTO

Larry Fitzgerald has fond childhood memories of his mom's pot roast served over rice. Here is the Candelaria twist on the Fitzgerald favorite.

SERVES 6–8

INGREDIENTS

Beef Pot Roast

3–3½ pounds boneless beef chuck roast

2 tablespoons avocado oil

1 large celery stalk, chopped

1 14.5-ounce can diced, Italian-style tomatoes

4 garlic cloves, smashed

1 bay leaf, 3 sprigs fresh thyme, 2 sprigs rosemary, and a sprig of fresh sage, tied together

4 carrots, peeled and cut into large sections

¾ cup red wine

1 medium yellow onion, minced

1 tablespoon flour or gluten-free flour

2 tablespoons water

⅛ to ¼ teaspoons salt and pepper, to taste

Italian flatleaf parsley

Porcini Mushroom Risotto

¼ cup unsalted butter

¼ cup olive oil

3 cups reconstituted dried porcini mushrooms, diced

3 cups diced button mushrooms

1 cup chopped onion

1 sprig rosemary

1½ cups arborio rice

¾ cup Pinot Grigio white wine

1 quart chicken stock

salt and ground black pepper, to taste

½ cup grated Parmesan cheese

PREPARATION

Beef Pot Roast

1. Rinse beef and pat dry with paper towels. Season with salt and pepper. Using the sauté setting on the Instant Pot, heat the oil and brown both sides of the beef, 5–6 minutes. Remove from heat and set aside on a plate.

2. Leaving the setting on sauté, add wine and celery and cook for 2–3 minutes. Then add the tomatoes, garlic, and herb bundle. Turn off the sauté function.

3. Set the browned beef on top of the sauce. Cover the Instant Pot and lock the lid securely. Set the pressure level to high and cook for 1 hour and 15 minutes.

4. When the cooking is done, release the pressure and move the roast to a plate or cutting board, and tent with foil to keep warm.

5. Add the carrots and chopped onions to the Instant Pot and lock the lid. Set on manual/pressure and cook for 4 minutes. Use the quick release and set unit to sauté and simmer.

6. Place water and flour in a small jar with a lid and shake thoroughly to dissolve flour. Add to wine sauce in Instant Pot, stir, and simmer until thickened, 2–4 minutes.

7. Cut the meat across the grain and place the meat into a large bowl or deep platter, pouring the carrots, onions, and wine sauce over the meat. Garnish with parsley and serve the porcini mushroom risotto on the side, also garnished with the chopped parsley.

Porcini Mushroom Risotto

1. Reconstitute the dried porcini mushrooms in water set to simmer in a saucepan, about 15 minutes. Remove the mushrooms by straining and reserve the liquid. Mince the softened mushrooms.

2. Select the sauté function on the Instant Pot and add butter and olive oil; stir until butter melts, about 2 minutes. Add diced button mushrooms; cook, stirring occasionally, until slightly softened, about 3 minutes. Stir in the diced porcini mushrooms and onion; cook for 2 minutes. Add rosemary sprig; cook for 1 minute.

3. Stir rice into the pot until each grain is coated with the butter-olive oil mixture, about 2 minutes. Pour in the wine and simmer for 3 minutes. Pour in chicken stock, stirring to scrape the sides of the pot. Simmer for 1 minute.

4. Close and lock the lid. Turn the venting knob to seal. Select high pressure according to manufacturer's instructions; set timer for 6 minutes. Allow 10–15 minutes for pressure to build.

5. When finished, tap venting knob with a wooden spoon to do a quick release. Remove lid when pressure is released, about 5 minutes.

6. Stir risotto until creamy, about 1 minute. Discard rosemary sprig. Season with salt and pepper. Stir in Parmesan cheese until melted and combined. Serve on the side of the pot roast and garnish with the chopped parsley.

Mark Candelaria, Meredith Thomson, and Larry Fitzgerald enjoy the annual Fitzgerald Foundation Dinner, "Fitz's Supper Club."

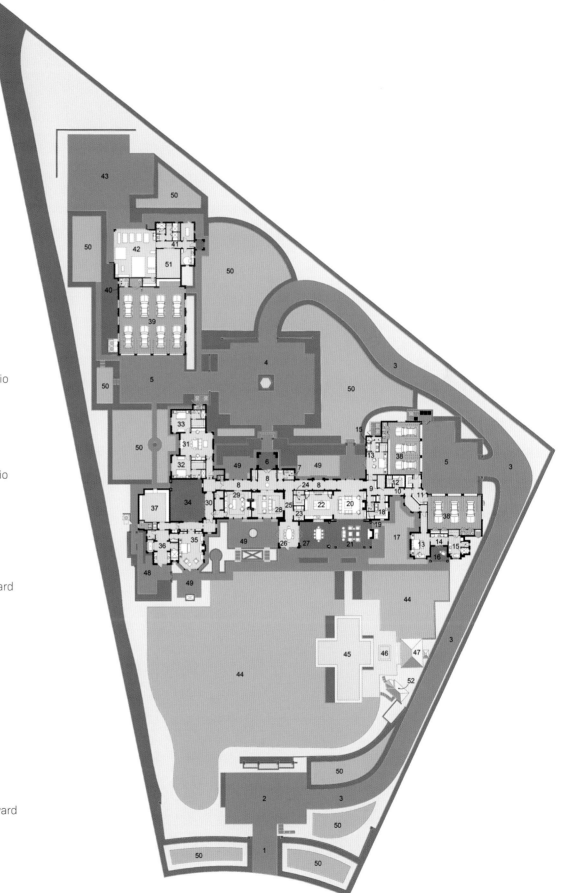

1 Arrival
2 Motorcourt
3 Driveway
4 Guest arrival
5 Auto court
6 Entry
7 Powder room 1
8 Gallery
9 Vestibule
10 Hall 2
11 Mudroom
12 Manager's office
13 Junior bedroom
14 Junior entry
15 Junior bath
16 Junior covered patio
17 Courtyard
18 Laundry
19 Powder room 2
20 Family room
21 Family room covered patio
22 Kitchen
23 Butler's pantry
24 Walk-in pantry
25 Dining hall
26 Dining room
27 Dining room covered patio
28 Living room
29 Office
30 Bedroom gallery
31 Kids study
32 Bedroom 2
33 Bedroom 3
34 Primary bedroom courtyard
35 Primary bedroom
36 Primary bath
37 Primary closet
38 Garage
39 Car collection
40 Powder bath 3
41 Owner's retreat
42 Gym
43 Sports court
44 Play lawn
45 Pool
46 Spa
47 Pool ramada
48 Primary bathroom courtyard
49 Terrace
50 Garden
51 Golf simulator
52 Pool folly

Larry Fitzgerald Residence • Floor Plan

APPENDIX

Project Data

CLEMMENSEN / GERDTS AND MCKINNEY RESIDENCE

Location: Paradise Valley, Arizona
Original Clients: Larry and Carol Clemmensen
New Owners: Mary Gerdts and Douglas McKinney
Completed: 2011
Size: 15,871 square feet
Architect: Mark Candelaria, AIA
Builder: Greg Hunt, GM Hunt Builders, Phoenix
Interior Designer: Donna Vallone, Vallone Design, Scottsdale, Arizona
Landscape Designer: Jeff Berghoff, Berghoff Design Group, Scottsdale, Arizona
Lighting Designer: Walter Spitz, Creative Designs in Lighting, Phoenix

MESSMER RESIDENCE

Location: Paradise Valley, Arizona
Current Owners: Matt and Brittany Messmer
Completed: September 2013
Size: 8,566 square feet
Architect: Mark Candelaria, AIA, principal; Jeffrey Kramer, AIA, project manager
Builder: John Schultz, Schultz Development, Scottsdale, Arizona
Interior Designer: David Miller, David Michael Miller Associates, Scottsdale, Arizona
Landscape Designer: Jeff Berghoff, Berghoff Design Group, Scottsdale, Arizona
Lighting Designer: Walter Spitz, Creative Designs in Lighting, Phoenix

SILVERLEAF ESTATE

Location: Scottsdale, Arizona
Completed: 2014
Size: 13,435 square feet
Architect: Mark Candelaria, AIA
Builder: Anthony Salcito, Salcito Custom Homes, Scottsdale, Arizona
Interior Designer: David Miller, David Michael Miller Associates, Scottsdale, Arizona
Landscape Designer: Jeff Berghoff, Berghoff Design Group, Scottsdale, Arizona
Lighting Designer: Walter Spitz, Creative Designs in Lighting, Phoenix

ITALIAN-MEDITERRANEAN VILLA

Location: Scottsdale, Arizona
Completed: 2013
Size: 14,752 square feet
Architect: Mark Candelaria, AIA
Builder: John Schultz, Schultz Development, Scottsdale, Arizona
Interior Designer: Kimberly Colletti, KC Design Group, Scottsdale, Arizona
Landscape Designer: Jeff Berghoff, Berghoff Design Group, Scottsdale, Arizona
Lighting Designer: Walter Spitz, Creative Designs in Lighting, Phoenix

HISTORIC JOHN M. ROSS TUDOR HOME

Location: Phoenix
Completed: 2012
Size: 6,981 square feet
Architect: Mark Candelaria, AIA
Builder: Nancy Brunkhorst, Nance Construction, Scottsdale, Arizona
Interior Designer: Niki Saulino, Vallone Design, Scottsdale, Arizona
Landscape Designer: Jeff Berghoff, Berghoff Design Group, Scottsdale, Arizona

WYSEL RESIDENCES

Location: Silverleaf, Scottsdale, Arizona; and Montecito, California
Clients: Glen and Lisa Wysel
Completed: 2008 (Silverleaf), 2013 (Montecito)
Size: 9,035 square feet (Silverleaf), 4,825 (Montecito)
Architect: Mark Candelaria, AIA, principal; Jeff Kramer, AIA, project manager
Builder: Ed West, West Development and Construction (Silverleaf)
Interior Designer: Charles Glover, Charles Glover Interiors (Silverleaf); Donna Vallone, Vallone Design, Scottsdale, Arizona (Montecito)
Landscape Designer: Puck Erikson, Arcadia Studio, Phoenix (Montecito)

GAGE RESIDENCE

Location: Scottsdale, Arizona
Clients: Jennifer and Matt Gage
Completed: 2016
Size: 7,758 square feet
Architect: Mark Candelaria, AIA
Interior Designer: Isabel Dellinger-Candelaria and Nikka Bochniak, Earth and Images, Phoenix
Landscape Designer: Jeff Berghoff, Berghoff Design Group, Scottsdale, Arizona

LANGE RESIDENCE

Location: Paradise Valley, Arizona
Clients: David and Linda Lange
Completed: 2015
Size: 5,707 square feet
Architect: Mark Candelaria, AIA
Builder: John Schultz, Schultz Development, Scottsdale, Arizona
Interior Designer: Claire Ownby, Ownby Design, Scottsdale, Arizona
Lighting Designer: Walter Spitz, Creative Designs in Lighting, Phoenix

SCHULTZ RESIDENCES

Location: Paradise Valley, Arizona
Clients: John and Denise Schultz
Completed: 2015
Size: 6,363 square feet
Architect: Mark Candelaria, AIA, principal; Jeffrey Kramer, AIA, project manager
Builder: John Schultz, Schultz Development, Scottsdale, Arizona
Interior Designer: Caroline DeCesare, DeCesare Design Group, Mesa, Arizona
Landscape Designer: Jeff Berghoff, Berghoff Design Group, Scottsdale, Arizona

JOHNSON RESIDENCE

Location: Paradise Valley, AZ
Clients: Steve and Donna Johnson
Completed: 2018
Size: 8,566 square feet
Architect: Mark Candelaria, AIA, principal; Mathew Grove, project manager
Builder: John Schultz, Schultz Development, Scottsdale, Arizona
Interior Designer: Anita Lang, IMI Design, Scottsdale, Arizona
Landscape Designer: Russell Greey, Greey | Pickett, Scottsdale, Arizona
Lighting Designer: Walter Spitz, Creative Designs in Lighting, Phoenix

LERNER RESIDENCE

Location: Scottsdale, Arizona
Clients: Gil and Phyllis Lerner
Completed: 2019
Size: 8,277 square feet
Architect: Mark Candelaria, AIA, principal
Builder: Jim Manship, Manship Builders, Carefree, Arizona
Imported Doors and Millwork: Gabriele Belli, Porte del Passato, Umbria, Italy
Landscape Architect: Eric Gilliland, Gilliland Design, Phoenix, Arizona

LARRY FITZGERALD RESIDENCE

Location: Paradise Valley, AZ
Original Clients: Larry Fitzgerald
New Owners: Mr. & Mrs. Michael Michelson
Completed: 2019
Size: 14,787 square feet
Architect: Mark Candelaria, AIA, principal; Meredith Thomson, AIA, project manager
Builder: John Schultz, Schultz Development, Scottsdale, Arizona
Landscape Designer: Jeff Berghoff, Berghoff Design Group, Scottsdale, Arizona
Lighting Designer: Walter Spitz, Creative Designs in Lighting, Phoenix
Kitchen and Millwork Designer: Christopher Peacock, Christopher Peacock, Greenwich, Connecticut

ACKNOWLEDGMENTS

I want to say a special thank you to coauthor David M. Brown and my daughter, Tiffany Candelaria, both of whom put an incredible amount of time, effort, and passion into the production of this book. I so enjoyed our teamwork and weekly Zoom calls along the way. Thanks also to my wife, Isabel, who has inspired me to go for it every day and encourages me and loves me despite the long hours it takes to be an architect. A big thanks to our clients who graciously opened and shared these amazing homes and entrusted us to design their dream homes. Finally, to my three partners, Evelyn Jung, Meredith Thomson, AIA, and Tim Mathewson, who are not only entrusted collaborators in this endeavor we call architecture, but more importantly, dear friends. Thank you!

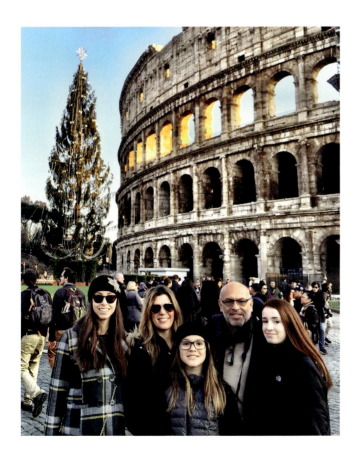

Mark and family in Italy in 2015, *from left to right*: Tiffany, Isabel Dellinger-Candelaria, Sophia, Mark, and Isabella

ABOUT THE AUTHORS

Architect Mark Candelaria has designed homes of all styles across the world in his 40-year career. Established in 1999, Candelaria Design Associates has won numerous awards, including Pacific Coast Builders Conference 2011 Home of the Year, ARA Awards, Ranking Arizona #1 Residential Architecture Firm eleven years in a row, Masonry Excellence Awards, Houzz Awards, Master of the Southwest, and LUXE Red Awards. He has been featured in books, magazines, and TV shows, including his own series, Sketch, on the Design Network. Mark was the architect for the HGTV 2017 Smart Home and the first 3-D-printed, fully livable home in the US. He is a board member of Scottsdale Arts and also the Central Arizona chapter of Habitat for Humanity. In addition, Mark hosts a weekly podcast, *Inspiring Living*, leads annual international tour, and loves to cook for friends and clients.

During his four decades as a journalist, **David M. Brown** has interviewed legends including Jay Leno, Judy Collins, Joan Baez, Alice Cooper, Lynn Redgrave, and many others. He especially enjoys writing about the architects, artists, and community leaders who are his Arizona neighbors.